Americanism Versus Bolshevism

The Mayor of Seattle's Personal Account of Battling Militant Communism and Revolution in his City in 1918

By Ole Hanson

PANTIANOS
CLASSICS

Published by Pantianos Classics

ISBN-13: 978-1-78987-325-2

First published in 1920

Ole Hanson

Contents

Dedication

I dedicate this book to all Americans who love their country, revere its ideals, understand and support its institutions, and are willing to give their all in order that "our Government shall not perish from the earth."

I dedicate this book to them, caring not from what human breed they sprang, regardless of their length of residence, despite any difference in religious creed or political faith, only requiring that they place our country, the United States of America, First, Now and Forever!

Preface

I UNDERTOOK the writing of this book for the purpose of placing before the people of my country the truth in relation to bolshevism and its American manifestation, I.W.W.'ism; as well as stating in plain language just what the concept of Americanism means to me.

I am tired of reading rhetorical, finely spun, hypocritical, far-fetched excuses for bolshevism, communism, syndicalism, I.W.W.'ism! Nauseated by the sickly sentimentality of those who would conciliate, pander, and encourage all who would destroy our Government, I have tried to learn the truth and tell it in United States English of one or two syllables.

Every statement made, every principle enunciated, every record quoted, almost without exception, is taken from the records of the syndicalistic and bolshevistic organizations; from the columns of their magazines and propaganda newspapers; from their text books; from the lips of their leaders and from other authoritative sources, agreed upon and repeatedly quoted by their propagandists.

In searching the pages of its brief but eventful history I could find no more terrific indictment of bolshevism and I.W.W.'ism than its own authoritative records, which prove conclusively that bolshevism is the autocratic rule of the lowest, least intelligent, least able class who believe that by "direct action" and "force" they can terrorize our people into turning over to them the conduct, ownership, and control of everything. Strikingly ignorant, malignantly cruel, with no concept of history, with but an elementary knowledge of social production, with little productive capacity, with no constructive ability, this movement in our country would be ludicrous were it not for the sentimental, weak-minded followers who, steeped in idealism and fanaticism, really believe in a Bolshevik Utopia, where free milk will run in the water mains and life may be supported without toil, where knowledge may be gained without effort, and where the established truths of the centuries will be overthrown by soviet resolutions.

With syndicalism — and its youngest child, bolshevism — thrive murder, rape, pillage, arson, free love, poverty, want, starvation, filth, slavery, autocracy, suppression, sorrow and Hell on earth. It is a class government of the unable, the unfit, the untrained; of the scum, of the dregs, of the cruel, and of the failures. Freedom disappears, liberty emigrates, universal suffrage is abolished, progress ceases, manhood and womanhood are destroyed, decency and fair dealing are forgotten, and a militant minority, great only in their self-conceit, reincarnate under the *Dictatorship of the Proletariat* a greater tyranny than ever existed under czar, emperor, or potentate.

The anarchist was courageous; he risked his life to take a life. The nihilist was a wan, despite his crimes of violence; but the Bolshevist (the I.W.W.) is a sneak and a coward *per se,* made so by the absorption of a propaganda which teaches violence of every description, advocates sabotage in the darkness, always, everywhere, saying: *"Do this deed. Terrorize the majority, but take care of your own worthless hide!"* Morally debauching every member by the teachings of cowardice and hate, the propagandists have used the ignorant and the mattoid and the moron for their foul purposes.

The American bolshevists (I.W.W.) fired wheat fields when our army needed wheat, put dead rats and mice in canned food, spiked logs in order to destroy machinery and fellow workmen, set forest fires, placed emery dust in machinery, burned down mills and logging camps, killed vineyards, and did every other damnable and cowardly thing, always taking care that their own life and liberty were safe.

Their real and avowed purpose is the overthrow of all order and government and the making of our country an experimental station for the purpose of trying out the blind vagaries and nightmares of the intellectual pismires and spittoon philosophers who would then become the autocrats in control of all things.

In this book I have briefly sketched the history of syndicalism in France, Germany, England, Russia, and the United States. I believe I have conclusively proven that the syndicalist, whether called bolshevist or I.W.W., is simply a revolutionary criminal; that each and every one teaches the commission of crime, that each and every one commits crime in the exact proportion as his courage and opportunity permit. The methods of syndicalism consist of force, direct action, sabotage, strike after strike, in order to foment class hatred, and then the general strike which if successful brings revolution.

The last part of the book is devoted to a discussion and explanation of the cures for bolshevism. In my constructive programme I have discussed Americanism and Americanization, selective immigration, education and educators, private rights, social legislation, deportation of aliens, punishment of citizens, and universal service.

A government which will not defend itself cannot stand. We have had enough of weakness, conciliation, and pandering. We must run the United States of America primarily for the United States of America.

America First!

Ole Hanson.

Chapter One - Why and How I Became Mayor of Seattle

WHEN I came to Seattle in 1902, I pitched my tent on Beacon Hill, a close-in, non-settled part of the city. The first night I arrived I stood on the hill and saw the child-city spread out before me. Below me to the west were the tide-lands covered with bulrushes, with an occasional street on stilts running over them; to the north was the city ablaze with light, with small buildings, narrow streets, a station house for a depot, and hills and hills covered with forests. Around the fire that night I told the curious who had gathered to watch the strangers that we had come to Seattle to make it our home, to be a part of its growth, and that some day I would be its mayor. Of course they laughed at the idea of the red-headed stranger with his team and covered wagon becoming the mayor of their city of 100,000 people. Laughter and ridicule have never bothered me, as I have always believed that if one wants to do anything bad enough, he can do it, and that it is just as easy to fish for whales as for minnows. Man is the only animal who can laugh and surely is the only one who ought to be laughed at. Anyhow, it is always easy to convert the man who laughs.

We built a home on Beacon Hill and lived there for many years, until my family increased so in size that we outgrew the house and spread out into two tent-houses. Then my wife, woman-like, insisted on securing a home with fourteen rooms. She said, in order to house the family, but verily, I believe, in order to have more work to do. While we now have a larger home, every now and then I return to the old spot to relive, as it were, one of the happiest periods of my life. And how we worked to plan and then build that first home! I dug the holes and planted the trees, brought the climbing rose-bush from Oregon, the birch from California, the magnolia from Florida. Really, you know, I like the old place best, and some day perhaps, when the boys and girls have gone out into the world, if I have money enough, I may buy it back and live there again. But we wander.

About Christmas time in 1917 people in Seattle began to look around for a mayor. They said they wanted a war-mayor and were tired of the old campaign issues. No one came and asked me to become a candidate, but folks generally conceded that if I made up my mind to run, I would win. Few ever ask an independent free man to seek office! Usually those who ask you to run want something *an honest man cannot grant!*

I happened, one evening, to go up to look at the old place and as I stood on the same promontory where I unhitched the team seventeen years before, I saw, instead of dank, stagnant tide-lands and bulrushes, hundreds of magnificent buildings; the waterfront was ablaze with thousands of lights; the furnaces lit up the heavens, and the shipyards fringing the bay looked like one great vessel with ropes and spars and with thousands of little things called men swarming about them. Some of the great hills were gone, washed away to replace the ooze of the ocean with solid land — and where were the forests? Cut down, sawed up, and in their places stood thousands of homes.

Seattle, at that time, had 400,000 people living in homes, many of which I had helped to build. For the first time in years real-estate and building were active and my business was prosperous. I knew that during the war one could amass a fortune in Seattle who knew the building business as well as I did. But our boy, our first born, was suffering from throat trouble. He was five feet nine and weighed but 109 pounds. He was not well and could not serve. I wanted to help and do my share. My parents had come to this country from Norway. They came here wanting liberty, freedom, and a greater opportunity for themselves and their children. They found this country to be good, and never tired of telling us, in broken English, what a great country this was and how different from any other land in the world. They loved the United States and so do their children, every one. Both were dead, but I knew that could I ask their advice, they would say, "our country is at war. Others are going to the front, but you can serve at home. Do your duty!" lowed considerable money (for me), but my creditors were secured and I felt they could wait. Wanting to serve my country in some capacity, I determined that evening to run for mayor and if elected, to abandon my private business and stay on the job *during the war.*

I did not know whether I could be elected as the political fights in which I had participated had been bitter. My support of the direct primary, the eight-hour law for women, the eight-hour law for underground miners, and the workmen's compensation act, etc., had made me enemies, and when I forced the passage of the anti-racetrack gambling bill, which eliminated a gang of crooks from our midst, the grafters never forgave me. My fight on the red-light district during three city campaigns earned for me the opposition of that multitude of wretches who owned and rented property in the district as well as all the box-coated, pink-cuffed hangers on. The business community, just awakening to the righteousness of the measures for which I had fought, still regarded me as somewhat unsafe. The labour forces had never had any fault to find with my record, and I felt that the "old timers" would be for me while the "Reds" and anti-war faction would just as surely be against me. My hope of election, apparently, depended on the great middle class who had no axes to grind, wanted no special privileges, but simply desired a fair, square business administration, 100 per cent, loyal.

Soon after our country entered the war Camp Lewis was established near Tacoma, a city of 100,000, thirty-eight miles away. It was here that the soldiers were to be received, trained, and prepared for war. Upon the establishment of this camp, immediate friction arose between army officials and Seattle's city officials. Mayor Gill, since dead, was in office. He was attacked by the army officials for not "keeping the town clean" and because "sedition and treason were not suppressed"; because the "I.W.W. still continued their activities," and because "no soldier could visit Seattle without being handed anti-war literature and hearing speeches against the Government." It was also openly charged that "Seattle was infested with itinerant women who, reeking with disease, were spreading the same amongst the soldiery." Army officials said that "the I.W.W. propaganda was German propaganda and that the women were oft-times German agents, paid with German money to destroy the health of the soldiers, and that the whole thing was a conspiracy against Uncle Sam and not just a 'happenstance.'" Notice was given to Mayor Gill to remove his chief of police and clean up. Gill told them to go to ___ and insisted that the town was clean. It was not clean, but so far as morality was concerned, it was certainly as clean as Tacoma. The Mayor of Tacoma, however, agreed to cooperate, and as I understand it Gill did not.

One morning Seattle awoke to find that a "ban" had been placed on the city of Seattle and no soldier or officer or any one connected with the army could enter our city except on army business. This was by order of General Greene in charge of Camp Lewis. It was a terrific blow to our civic pride, and every effort was made by determined citizens to cause Mr. Gill to change his mind, remove his chief of police, and do as the army officials dictated. After six weeks of national disgrace for our city Mayor Gill did remove the chief and appointed in his stead Joel F. Warren, who had been in the Government Secret Service.

At the request of the Government, Mayor Gill then instituted a quarantine station for diseased men and women under the supervision of Commissioner of Health Dr. J. S. McBride. From that time on (and we are still continuing it), when men and women were arrested for certain misdemeanors, they were given a thorough examination, including the Wasserman and Noguchi blood tests, and if found infected, were quarantined and kept away from society until all trace of the malady had disappeared.

There was a great deal of dissatisfaction with the conduct of affairs at the City Hall, for years every campaign having been conducted on police issues. We really did not elect a mayor to conduct the affairs of a great business institution, such as Seattle had become, but to become a kind of glorified chief of police. Great issues were forgotten every time and petty police disputes were in everyone's mouth. A ten-cent poker game received more headlines than did the municipal light and power plant. The trials of alleged grafting policemen filled our dailies while city business ran any old way. The position of mayor was a trying one. With the city just emerging from its frontier past, some of the old ways persisted and the new laws were often resisted. One crowd or the other, *usually both,* were against the mayor!

Men fit to guide the destinies of the city either refused to neglect their private business or were thought unable to secure election. The next election was to be held March 5, 1918, and, as in the past, it was thought necessary to have a chance for success, that the candidate must either become subservient to Big Business or to the labour group. One or the other, politicians said, a candidate must have. One or the other, they said, a mayor must serve. I have always held a different theory. It has been my belief since a boy that a candidate for office, playing fair and square with all men, with no special interest to serve, could be elected, provided he was believed to be honest and could get *circulation.* I have helped demonstrate to the politicians very often in my lifetime that they really cannot run nominations or elections if the people are appraised of their intentions.

After reviewing this situation in my mind I went home and told my wife of my decision. She never favoured my political ventures, but this time she assented on account of the war. The next day the papers carried notice of my candidacy and things started to happen. I had no campaign committee — they usually talk and seldom work. I wanted no headquarters for political loafers. I wanted no paid workers — they are so often no good. My campaign was to be purely a truth-telling one. I would attack no opponent, but would tell the people what I would do if elected, not that someone else had done wrong. It was a new method in Seattle and consisted in telling the people: "If elected I will do this." I had never lied to the people and felt they would believe me. I engaged a stenographer and prepared my own printed matter.

The chairman of the Republican Central Committee announced his candidacy; a former prosecuting attorney entered the field; the president of the Municipal League filed, followed quickly by a young man who had held mass meetings denouncing vice and who believed himself to be a great man, but who had failed to convince others. Then came Mayor Gill seeking reelection.

About that time a delegation from the Central Labour Council called on me, tendering me the support of their 65,000 members, provided I would agree, upon my election, to let Joel F. Warren, chief of police, go.

I asked: "What's the matter with Warren?" They said: "Your record has always been fair; in the legislature and on the labour committee you were 100 per cent.; you fought the fight for better conditions, but Joel Warren at one time was a police officer during a strike over across the mountains. He does not suit us." I then asked: "What did he do?" After several evasive answers they replied: "He arrested and imprisoned the boys when they tried to raise a little hell." I then told them that I thought their statement was the best recommendation I had heard for Warren; that if he enforced and observed the law, he certainly would remain chief if I was elected. They then asked for the discharge of the fire chief, a man with an excellent record as an efficient fire fighter and whose reputation in the community was beyond reproach. As with the chief of police, I told them he would also remain if I was elected, provided, always, he did his duty. They left with threats on their lips and the next day a man named Bradford, who had been corporation counsel for the city, was chosen by the Central Labour Council Committee as their candidate. He had never done anything for labour; he had never accomplished much but quarrel for the city, but "Jim" was subservient to their wishes and would represent *them* if he became mayor.

At the last moment a millionaire shipping man filed his candidacy. That made eight, but upon reading the charter, a local paper found that the last candidate was ineligible because of his not having been an American citizen four years, so he withdrew. He was a very good man, able and courageous, and would have secured certain business support which I afterward received.

As soon as the filings closed and the campaign began, I issued my card containing my platform. It was brief, hence I quote it:

I stand for construction, not destruction; more factories and less lawsuits; a square deal to labour as well as capital; for a loyal, united Seattle, a Seattle free from turmoil, treason, and I.W.W. control.

Immediately I became the foe of the "inner circle" at the Labour Temple. Their propaganda factory worked to the utmost to convince the new workers that Hanson was a bad one. Believing that no "clique" could control the minds of the *thinkers in labour,* once they knew the truth, I immediately published a letter I had received from the past president of the State Federation of Labour, thanking me for my service to labour in the Legislature and saying: "You are 100 per cent, right."

With no paid campaign workers, I made a strenuous campaign through pamphlets and mass meetings. Three dailies came out for me and printed the truth, but the I.W.W. element worked night and day spreading their lies. One evening, as the campaign waxed hotter and hotter, and the Red element at the Labour Temple became more vicious in their attacks on me, I went before their weekly meeting. I told them: "I have not come before you for your votes or your support, but I have come here to tell you the truth about yourselves as well as review in brief my history in the state of Washington as far as it relates to labour." I then quoted from the official record as to my stand on the remedial and reform measures which had been agitated and sometimes enacted into law. In every instance the official documents and letters from their own officials showed conclusively that I had made the fight, spent my time and my money furthering the progress of labour. They sat in silence; once in a while one would applaud. James Duncan, one of the Reds and secretary of the Central Labour Council of whom I will have more to say later, tried to interrupt several times, fearing the effect of the truth on the upright and fair members of the council, but so interested were the auditors that he was promptly squelched. In closing I denounced the Reds, the I.W.W.'s and their kind, and said: "If elected I will clean you up (meaning the Reds) lock, stock, and barrel. You do not belong in this country. Your talk of revolution has no place where the majority can and does govern. You are fighting the best government yet conceived by man. I shall close every hall where the overthrow of our Government by force and violence is taught. You shall not parade with the Red Flag; you shall obey the law or you shall go to jail. Neither your leaders nor the leaders of the Chamber of Commerce shall control the city government. It shall be run for the benefit of all the people, not a particular class. You are against me because I am for the government you are against. You know there is nothing wrong with my labour record, but my government record is too loyal to suit you. I defy you and your kind. You make the most noise, but Seattle is loyal and will not stand for your control. I shall see the day when some of you that now hiss and jeer will do so behind prison walls." Within a year two of my hearers, Hulet M. Wells and Sam Sadler, were in the Federal Penitentiary and others who were present will surely follow when justice is done.

That meeting at the Labour Temple clinched my nomination. Truth is a powerful weapon if one can only give it circulation. From that meeting on, the rank and file asked the Red leaders questions *which they could not answer.* Within twenty-four hours loyal labour men and women called and proffered me their secret help. It meant ostracism for them openly to defy the men who controlled the Central Labour Council. For fifteen years I have always known how elections were going. I have my own method of taking a poll, and it has never failed me. This poll showed that I would lead in the primary, Bradford (candidate of the labour leaders) second, and Mayor Gill third, with the "great young man" last. And so it happened. Under our non-partisan election law the top two are nominated and then two weeks afterward the election takes place.

In the primary I received nearly one half of all the votes, although there were seven candidates. In the finals Mr. Bradford and his supporters endeavoured to offset the charge that the I.W.W.'s were backing him by claiming that his ancestors came over in the *Mayflower.* The *Mayflower* certainly must have had gutta-percha sides. His "ancestral father" claim did him little good, for I had a logger friend of mine poll the I.W.W. hall and the result was Bradford 180, Hanson none. This result was published and when the votes were counted on election day, Bradford was overwhelmingly defeated, and to the labour leaders' chagrin and surprise I carried dozens of precincts where no one but union workers lived! Union labour people are the same as you and I. They are for right just as you and I, and when the facts are before the rank and file no fairer jury could be desired.

On the same day I was elected mayor, Anna Louise Strong, who had been educated in Germany and was a member of the School Board, was recalled from that honourable position because of her antagonism to our Government, and she was recalled by almost exactly the same number of votes that elected me mayor. The same forces that supported me voted for her recall. The line was plainly drawn and most of the people took their stand on our side. The entire campaign against my election was because I stood with the Government at Washington, and the Reds knew that their anti-war activities would be suppressed, come what would.

I took my oath of office on March 5, 1918, and within a few days the very men who had fought my election tried to use "soft soap" in order to sway me from my path. The business community had supported me almost to a man and most of the old resident union men had done the same. Within a few

13

days the Chamber of Commerce, which I did not trust, offered to help me in any way they could. It was my opinion they would want something wrong; that they had ulterior motives, and the offer was but a bluff. But I am frank to say it was not. During my entire term of office the business community assisted me in every manner possible and *never tried to dictate the policy of the administration in a single particular.* They left me entirely alone, but when once embarked upon my course of action, I found helpers in every bank, factory, and business house in Seattle. The great rank and file of labour has supported my every endeavour, while on the other hand the labour misleaders came time and again for favours and privileges ranging from asking the discharge of department heads to getting out of jail men who had committed crime. I soon learned that overalls did not denote a greater degree of honesty than broadcloth. When I was in the Legislature, Big Business tried to run things; as mayor, I found the I.W.W. demanded control. The *Red employer* and the *Red employee* are interchangeable anarchists!

As soon as I came to get the "feel" of my new position I investigated the quarantine of men and women and demanded that the council give me better quarters to house them. This was *consistently refused on one plea or another until the date of my leaving office.*

I called a congress of the Northwest to consider the "vice" question from a new angle — the sanitary one. Doctor McBride, the Commissioner of Public Health, redoubled his efforts, and within ninety days after I became mayor, we *cut the rate of diseased soldiers drafted from Seattle* from four out of one hundred to one out of one hundred. The vice congress spread to other states and during the war Washington, Oregon, and Idaho, because of the quarantine of the infected, led the government list. In other words, fewer of our soldiers were found infected upon going to camp than those from any other part of the nation. Despite his wonderful work Doctor McBride became the target of every pacifist, every I.W.W., every pro-German, and every vice profiteer in the city. Everyone who was against the war was against the quarantine.

One man, who pulls teeth by day and practises law by night, had supported me for mayor, as I thought, because he believed I would serve the people. In reality, as I afterward learned, he supported me because he thought I would serve him and his crowd. He haunted my offices continually and waged an open fight against the quarantine station, and collected $1,100, under the guise of attorney fees, from five inmates, these particular inmates being the ones he was trying to have me release. One member of the City Council was his able assistant. Doctor McBride and myself worked with and under the direction of army physicians and to the last had their enthusiastic cooperation. I wondered at the opposition of the council member until his wife called at my home one evening and told me the unprintable story of their lives. Then I understood his opposition to compulsory treatment and quarantine. The reason the quarantine was fought was because *the men who fought it were either against our securing a healthy army, fit to fight, or were engaged in making profit from the unfortunates.*

As a mayor one learns too much of the vileness of men. I had never before really sensed what men would do for money. While the council refused a better place to house the prisoners, despite repeated requests, members of the council attacked us because the place was not sanitary. Hypocrisy could go no further!

Some day the Government will district the United States and meet this scourge by quarantining, treating, and curing all infected persons. Our experience proves that a few years of such procedure will practically wipe out these dread diseases. In the beginning of the quarantine more than eighty per cent. of the women and men arrested and examined were found to be infected. In six months' time less than forty per cent, were found infected, and in twelve months, less than ten per cent.

We treated many hundreds, but the greatest benefit came from the publicity which caused unarrested folk to secure treatment at once. The afflicted hurried to their physicians and took private treatment. I sent a questionnaire to some three hundred who were at one time in quarantine and there were no skilled or trained workers among them and only one that even claimed to have attended a high school. They were an ignorant, dirty, incompetent, uneducated crowd, whose mentality was on the average not as high as children of fourteen. They were mostly un-moral, not immoral. They were so ignorant, few realized what they were doing to the soldier boys; few indeed sensed the gravity of their condition at all, and almost invariably had no moral sense whatever. The war did one thing for the American people — it opened their eyes to this menace. Some day the Government will, as I have said, by a continuous, forceful campaign, clean it up.

The I.W.W. halls were still open, their propaganda was still being distributed, and many wondered why I had not closed them at once. I knew why. We waited until May 2nd, nearly six weeks after my election, for two reasons. One was to secure the names and addresses of all who were members of the I.W.W., and the other was to ascertain where they secreted their literature. The day after the European Labour Day, May 1st, we struck, and *closed every I.W.W. hall in Seattle and kept them closed.* We confiscated their literature, burned up what we did not turn over to the Government, and stopped every street meeting. Hall meetings were closed to everyone who preached overthrow of our Government by force and violence and we received the united support of the vast majority of the citizens of Seattle.

In the summer of 1918 the election of officers of the Central Labour Council took place. Robert L. Proctor and Hulet M. Wells, of whom the latter had been at one time socialist candidate for mayor and had already been convicted in the Federal Court for violating the Espionage Act, were opposing candidates. It was only after days and nights of hard work that Proctor finally was elected by a scant majority of 25 votes over Hulet M. Wells! Think of it! — a central labour council in an American city were able to marshal only 25 more votes for a loyal, able union man than for a man who openly proclaimed himself a bolshevist and who was even then under sentence.

15

For a time all was lovely with the leaders of the Central Labour Council. Fear of an outraged people kept them semi-silent. The rank of the union men came to see that I was fair and square, and upon the purchase of the street car lines by the city, the largest local union in the world, having 18,000 members, voted me an *honorary* membership and presented me with a silver membership card.

The committee that called upon me to present the card came to the mayor's office and my secretary took down what was said. Their spokesman said: "We present you this card as a token of our appreciation of your services during your life to labour; you have always stood firm and true for the man who toils. Last spring many of us supported your opponent; we feel we were mistaken and want to assure you that every act of yours has been satisfactory to us." I replied: "You are presenting me with honorary membership in your union. You say you do this because of my services to the cause of labour. I accept this card in the same spirit as I hope it is given, but feel that you are giving me this card because you happen to agree with what I have done and that the time may come when I will do something just as right but with which you will not agree. When that time comes, this card is ready and waiting for you, as I refuse, as mayor of Seattle, to serve any particular class in the community. I shall represent them all."

This occurred in September, 1918. On August 30, 1919, they had not called for the card. I then returned it to them with a letter which denounced their leaders; stated they (the leaders) had "entered into a coalition with the I.W.W.'s and planned for the overthrow of the Government at the time of the general strike; had planned to turn over the city government to a soviet approved by A. E. Miller, James Duncan, Anna Louise Strong, recalled school director; George F. Vandeveer, I.W.W. attorney; Wm. D. Haywood, national secretary of the I.W.W.; Leon Green, Russian anarchist, and Sam Sadler and Hulet M. Wells convicted seditionists." I expressed the hope "that the rank and file will, in the near future, remove from the positions of power the officers and leaders who so grossly misled and deceived the workers and by so doing proved themselves not only false to this country and my flag (not *their* flag), but also false to the true principles of labour unionism. Until that time arrives I cannot, as an American citizen who loves his country, retain even a card presented by an organization ruled by such men. The cause of labour has ever had and always will have my support, but no organization can supersede my loyalty to the United States."

One of my first acts as mayor was to cause a survey to be made of the cost of living and when the difference in cost over the pre-war period was ascertained, I recommended and succeeded in securing an increase of the city workers' minimum wage from $3.50 to $4.00 per day. Some months later we made another survey and increased common labour to $4.50 per day. Just before I left the mayor's office I recommended to the budget committee a raise of 12¼ per cent,, which was the exact increase in living costs from July 1, 1918, to July 1, 1919, in Seattle. The committee agreed to make the increase when the budget was passed. Skilled craftsmen were, of course, increased in proportion. It was impossible for the city government of Seattle to regulate the cost of living; all we could do was to keep track of the increased cost and see that the city's employees received a sufficient wage to live in decency and comfort. The dollar measure is so full of rubber that without taking into consideration what the dollar will buy, no fair wage can be established! Besides, a well-paid worker is not susceptible to the rainbow-hued promises of the bolshevists. I consider it not only good morals, but good business to give men what they are entitled to, without waiting for them to make a fight for it. If men secure increased remuneration for their services, after they have struck, or threatened to strike, they believe, and usually rightly so, that they *force the employer* to be fair. If the wage is increased without any such action, it proves to the worker that the employer thinks of somebody besides himself.

During the war a great need of men occurred in the shipyards, and in order to set a good example and assist the Government, I went to work in the yards after putting in most of the day in the mayor's office. While there I did a full day's work without any camouflage. It was hard work and the scant $4.00 a day was not enough money for the work and not enough for the labourer to live in decency and comfort. While in the shipyards I became acquainted with many good men and some bad ones. You did not have to ask a man whether he was a Red or not. The manner in which he worked showed that. If he was against the Government, he did as little as possible in as long a time as possible, and in as poor a manner as possible. If he was loyal and right, he did a fair day's work, looked the boss in the eye, and did not "soldier." In the main, however, the boys worked hard, but under the hulls the minority were continually agitating "taking over industry," "running things ourselves," and "joining the one big union."

The speakers sent out by the Government to the shipyards did a valuable work, no doubt, but it always seemed to me that they spread it on pretty thick. One would think, to listen to some of the spell-binders, that the shipyard workers were working for $30.00 per month, like the soldiers, and had all enlisted to serve the Government during the war for patriotic reasons. This was true of some but by no means true of all. Men went to work in the shipyards for different reasons — some to earn a living, some to assist Uncle Sam, others to escape the draft, and a considerable number simply to agitate against the Government and bring about chaos in our country. There is no use lying about these things. There were many bad men, many Revolutionists, and many slackers in the Government works everywhere, and there were many aliens and I. W.W.'s who spent a goodly share of their time talking and agitating against the Government they were receiving their bread and butter from. As a matter of fact, there were several thousand I. W.W.'s who had formerly operated in Butte, Montana, who came to work in the yards, feeling that they were secure from arrest in the larger and more cosmopolitan city of Seattle. A great many more came here from Arizona, Idaho, and California. Everyone knew that Seattle was the home nest — the headquarters — the central station — for their organization in the United States.

During the war a great many kept under cover through fear of prosecution and the draft law, but when the armistice was signed, anti-government activities increased overnight. A carefully planned propaganda of discontent was spread among the workers, especially in the shipyards. The increased cost of living, the fact that many of the men were away from their families, and living in over-crowded quarters, aided the agitators. It was a strange sight to see men from Russia, the land of tyranny and poverty, preaching against the Government of the land where they had sought refuge. The doctrine of syndicalism was especially effective with the young men in the yards. American-born youths. with loyal fathers, accepted, believed, and assisted the propaganda.

The Government and the workers throughout the Union had agreed on a peaceful adjustment of all differences worked out by the Macy Board, and this governmental body now became the target for attack. In November, 1918, the officers of the unions asked that the workers vote for a strike unless the Macy Board agreed to their demands when they journeyed east. The men in Seattle understood that this was to be but a bluff" to force the Macy Board to grant them higher wages, despite a definite and certain agreement which was in effect at that time. No other vote than this vote, which was to arm the officers with a bluff", was ever taken before the shipyard strike was called three months later.

I felt that some of the workers in the yards were not receiving sufficient wages. This was undoubtedly true of the common labourers — but it was not the wages or conditions that caused the leaders to agitate the strike. It was because of a desire on their part to foment hatred, suspicion, and discontent to such a degree that the workers would first make impossible demands; then call a general strike, establish a soviet, and start the flame of revolution in this country, with the hope and plan of the ultimate destruction of the Government and the establishment in its stead of bolshevism, pure and undefiled, with its consequent red terror and tyranny. But few of the shipyard workers knew of this conspiracy. They were simply taught to hate their employer; to hate the Macy Board; to defy the Macy award, and to refuse to work for the Macy scale.

The employer in this case was practically the Government, as all contracts were governmental contracts and the wages were fixed by a governmental body. Everywhere — on the street cars, at work, at home — the agitators told of the fabulous receipts of the shipyard owners, nothing being said of the great overhead, or of the men in the yards who did no more than half a day's work for a full day's pay. Nothing was said either of the great war taxes imposed by the Government. The shipyard owners had no interest in holding down the pay of the men. Under their contract with the Government, any increase in the cost of labour meant a consequent increase in the prices paid them by the Government for their ships. Without the Government's sanction, no raise in wages could be made. Agitators everywhere talked of taking over industries and "firing" the bosses, but condemnation of governmental action was their main theme.

This state of unrest, of hatred, of lies and suspicion was fanned every day by a newspaper called the Seattle *Union Record*. This paper had formerly been a weekly, but upon the influx of the workers and the consequent increase in the labour unions it was transformed into a daily. It is not a union paper, but a sheet which sometimes by clever insinuation, and sometimes openly, preaches internationalism, hatred of government, and revolution.

Its editor, A. B. Ault, at one time worked for a living, but now heads one of the most radical newspapers in the country, one which will probably be suppressed by the Government.

There is no backache in his job, or headache either. Backache comes from toil — headache, from thought! He refuses to toil and has not the tools with which to think. He was chosen editor of the paper because of his well-known revolutionary tendencies and because strong-minded men knew that he would obey them without question. The office force of the *Record* is as Red as their headlines. The *Record's* leading editorial and special writer was and is Anna Louise Strong, recalled by the outraged citizens of Seattle from the position she so dishonoured on the School Board the same day I was elected mayor.

At one time I visited the office of the *Record* and found it in an uproar of joy. Theodore Roosevelt was dead! It was January 6, 1919, my birthday. I asked: "Why the jubilation?" And Ault shouted, "Roosevelt is dead, he stood in our way." That night the paper carried an editorial on Roosevelt's death from which I quote a part:

Theodore Roosevelt Is Dead

Theodore Roosevelt is dead...His outlook was never very subtle or penetrating...Roosevelt lived to see the progressive movement, which he once championed, moved so far past him that he was driven to closer and closer arraignment with the most reactionary forces in this nation. His conception of society's friendship, never very fundamental, was clouded more and more by his own egotism, played upon by those big interests which know so well what motives to stress in order to gain their end.

We must admit the fact that his death at the present moment removes one of the greatest obstacles to permanent peace throughout the world...But they will hardly find quickly another mouth-piece who could so convincingly mislead the people of this country...

From that day to this I have never visited the office of the *Record*. The unclean atmosphere of treason stifles me, and besides, when Ault made his statement in relation to the death of one of the greatest men of his time — a real American — I said things which were true and forceful, but which precludes my seeing Ault again unless perchance I could gaze on him in stripes.

In order to show the spirit and hypnosis of the *Record* staff, I will relate another incident which occurred when I met a lady reporter who worked for the paper. She said: "Mr. Mayor, we have sure got the goods on John Miller." (Miller is our Congressman.) I said: "What has John done now?" She said: "He just denounced the Red Flag." I said: "That ought to boost him." She replied by saying: "Not with our readers." The Reds really believed they were in a majority and that Mr. Miller had destroyed his political future. Wellington once said: "I mistrust the judgment of every man in a case in which his own wishes are concerned." The death of Roosevelt gave great courage to the foes of our Government. His moral influence and his fearless stand against wrong were a greater influence than most of us can realize.

Chapter Two - Agitation of the Industrial Workers of the World Culminates in Shipyard Strike

About the time of Col. Roosevelt's death and my visit to the *Record* office the I.W.W.'s became even more threatening in their attitude toward the city authorities. One evening E. I. Chamberlain, a general secretary of the I.W.W., called me on the 'phone and demanded the release of all prisoners in the city jail who belonged to his order, and also a permit to open the I.W.W. halls. Of course I told him "No." He then said: "Do you want your jail overcrowded with I.W.W.'s?" My reply to his question was that our jail was a little overcrowded, but we would always find sufficient quarters to house "all law breakers." As a parting shot he said: "Well, the battle is on; we'll show you."

Apparently, orders went out to increase I.W.W. activities. The police next raided an office in the Pacific Block, and a great quantity of new literature aimed at the Government was confiscated and destroyed. I felt that trouble could not long be averted and that it was necessary to have a larger police force, but the Public Safety Committee of the council on January 8, 1918, had refused the request of the chief of police, endorsed by myself, for more police. Councilman Erickson leading the opposition.

A great throng of women from all parts of the city then went before the committee and told them of outrages being perpetrated in the suburbs, but it was of no avail — the committee again turned the request down. After the committee had been attacked and ridiculed in the public press, however, the council itself granted a small increase. But there were other ways to get police without securing the votes of such men as Erickson. When the time of necessity came, I appointed emergency police, many of them, and an appropriation was made for their payment by the votes of all the council, including Erickson.

With additional recruits pouring into the shipyards daily, the activities of the I.W.W.'s on the outside were redoubled, if such a thing were possible. In the early part of January, 1919, five leading members of the I.W.W. met in secrecy in Room 310, Collins Building — the headquarters of the Metal Trades Council — and after carefully studying the procedure used in Russia, formed among themselves a soviet, which was to be called the "Soldiers, Sailors, and Workmen's Council." Several revolutionary speeches were made and it so happened that every word was overheard, except the words of one man who was clever enough to hold his hand over his mouth as he spoke, so that his words were but an indistinct mumble.

Thus a soviet came into existence by secrecy and stealth with only five members present. It was decided to call a great mass meeting on the corner of Fourth Avenue and Virginia Street. The meeting was to be called "on behalf of Russia," as a camouflage, then was to be turned into an organization meeting of the "Soldiers, Sailors, and Workmen's Council." A great parade was to be formed which, following the Red Flag, would march to the city jail and release the prisoners. An advertisement appeared in the *Union Record,* giving notice of the meeting. Circulars were distributed all over the city, stating that Hulet M. Wells, already convicted of sedition and out on bail, would be one of the speakers and Mr. ___, of Canada, would be the other. On some of the circulars it was stated that "The meeting is to be held under the auspices of the Metal Trades, Central Labour Council and Hope Lodge No. 79, Machinists."

Knowing what the soviet plans were, I was surprised at the signature to the circular, and in company with Councilman Robert B. Hesketh, a union labour loyalist, I went to the Central Labour Council, and there the business agent of the council informed me that the Central Labour Council knew nothing of the meeting. We then called on A. L. Miller, one of the heads of the Metal Trades Council (since suspended by his International Union), and he said he knew nothing of the meeting. I made proper police arrangements, instructing the officers not to interfere with the meeting, but to allow things to come to a head. The police authorities marshalled their men in the assembly room and waited. Word had reached the conspirators that we were prepared, and the mysterious speaker from Canada did not appear. Hulet M. Wells could not be present because of *tonsillitis!* S. W. Brooks, under order of deportation by the Federal authorities, was chairman of the meeting. Brooks then called for "fellow workers" to volunteer and distribute propaganda literature, appealing to the soldiers and sailors to join the ranks of those who would "put down industrial autocracy at home." As stated by the *Seattle Post-Intelligencer* on January 13, 1919, Walker C. Smith, author of "Sabotage," and an I.W.W. leader, followed, demanding "release of all political prisoners" and calling the naval intelligence staff "a bunch of scab herders." In speaking of the necessity of changing the Government, he said: "If our Government cannot be changed without bloodshed, let bloodshed come," and concluded with the words: "Hail to the bolsheviki, hail to the Revolution." A. V. Brown, the next speaker, said to the men in the shipyards: "You men are going to be discharged. But when the time comes, refuse to quit. Stay on the job. Tell them if there is not enough work for all, the working day must be shortened to six hours." Thousands of circulars were passed out at the meeting, calling on the soldiers and sailors to join their ranks.

After the speakers had concluded, several "soap-boxers" and alien speakers moved out into the street and in a few minutes several meetings were in progress and obstructing traffic. This was forbidden by city ordinance and the police immediately asked that the meetings be held on an adjoining lot so as not to obstruct the street.

Just then a loaded lumber wagon came along with a red flag swinging from the rear end — and this on Sunday, the day of rest! I now quote from the *Seattle Daily Times*, January 13th:

Someone raised the cry: "There she is! There's the only flag!" In a flash the cry was taken up. The wagon momentarily stopped while almost all took off their hats to the emblem of Bolshevism and someone started the chorus of "The Red Flag," an I.W.W. battle cry...Mutterings grew to loud cries and a violent attitude of the surging crowd.

Spying a man - since declared by the police to be Walker Smith, a noted I.W.W. agitator - gathering a crowd about him...Captain Searing, who was directing the splitting up of the throng, broke away from the other officers and dashed through the mob toward the man, said to be Smith.

"I wanted to nip in the bud any further demonstration and stop the parade he was endeavouring to form before it could get under way and make such a mob that we would have difficulty in handling it," said Captain Searing afterward in explaining his action. "I wanted to get them before they had a chance to get us," he added.

The police captain had not quite reached his objective when the persons surrounding the would-be parade marshal attacked Searing. The latter declared later he couldn't pick out a single person who had attacked him, save one woman who was trying to strike him with her fists and an umbrella...Captain Searing early became the centre of the fighting, but was saved from serious injury by the arrival of squad after squad of police...Patrolman Bert Houck pursued a man through the crowd who was advancing on Captain Searing with a large pocketknife.

Several of the radicals were arrested "while proclaiming...their disrespect for the American flag and this Government. One of them, W. I. Fisher, was shouting 'Down with Democracy' it is alleged, when Sergeant Ballinger of the military police gathered him in."

As the mob was broken up they cast slurs at several men in the army and navy and marine service with whom they came in contact. Continuing, the *Times* said:

In these mêlées Sergeant Moore, in charge of the Fort Lawton provost guard, was struck in the mouth after he had arrested a man who had been discharged from the army on December 19th last. This prisoner, it was alleged, had taken off his hat to the red flag on the lumber wagon and was loudly declaring his "wobblyism" (I.W.W.'ism) and lack of respect for the Stars and Stripes.

Parading without a permit had always been forbidden, and as Police Captain Searing ran into the centre of the street and ordered the paraders to break ranks, his answer was a blow in the face which broke his nose and knocked him to the pavement. Immediately a dozen Reds joined in the assault, but he finally succeeded in regaining his feet and with the aid of his men fought clear of the crowd. When the provost guard or police arrested one of their assailants, others fought to release him.

In commenting upon the attack made upon Sergeant Morris of the Marines, the *Times* added:

The most exciting incident next to the attack on Captain Searing was the assault on Sergeant Morris of the U.S. Marines. He was struck in the mouth by a man who later gave his name as Leo Polishuk, a Russian labourer, twenty years old. The marine captured his assailant at Fourth Avenue and Pike Street and was taking him toward an alley "to give him a trial and punish him on the spot" when the city police hurried up and through the crowd, which was threatening to take Morris's prisoner from him.

Among those who tried to rescue Polishuk from the marine was Leo Udcovisky, forty-five years old, a Russian. Sergeant (Jack) Sullivan (Seattle soldier and loyalist), who was going to the marine's assistance, grabbed Udcovisky and turned him around. The Russian kicked him, and while the soldier was recovering from this blow his assailant, it is alleged, tried to strike him with an iron bar.

As the Russian started away from the scene, hurrying down the alley toward Union Street, Sullivan painfully followed, never losing sight of him. In front of the Post Office Building he caught up to him and made him prisoner.

It was a free-for-all fight before it was over, but when things commenced to be fairly equal, the cowardly Reds "hunted their holes," as they always do and always will do. There is no courage in them! Their teachings have taken all sacrifice and ability to battle out of them! They never won a single fight with the police while I was mayor. Given 200 Seattle blue coats and 1,000 Reds — the Reds run!

A total of thirteen men were arrested and when one was asked what his nationality was he said: "I am an American, and ashamed of it." Thus ended, in the Reds' defeat, the first open battle between the forces of law and order and the I.W.W. in Seattle.

The well-laid plans of the "Soldiers, Sailors, and Workmen's Council" could not be carried out on account of the help given the police by the loyal citizens and returned soldiers. In the entire crowd of Reds, there was but one returned soldier.

The *Union Record* the next day, in flaring headlines, denounced the police for enforcing the law. It also published an editorial, calling the police "Prussians," and abused the chief.

The next day, January thirteenth, I made the following statement:

Order will be maintained. Laws will be enforced. Riot and disorder will be suppressed.

23

The men arrested were found guilty and police sentences imposed.

On the following Wednesday I went to the meeting held in the Central Labour Council in order to secure statements of any specific usurpation or abuse of authority on the part of the police. When I arrived, there was, as usual, but a small attendance of Central Labour Council members, the vacant seats being filled by I.W.W.'s who were not members. These men voted, however, on motion after motion, as did the Reds who filled the gallery. The speakers simply denounced the police and all in authority, but did not present for consideration a single, specific instance where a policeman or provost guard had not observed, as well as enforced, the plain law.

When my name was mentioned, a man sitting among a crowd of I. W.W.'s and bearded Russians (all, by the way, wearing red neckties), shouted, "Let's hang Hanson." I was unable to reach him before he disappeared in the crowd. Upon leaving the hall, several I.W.W.'s blocked my path and started an argument. Although alone I was fully prepared to protect myself, but the argument did not last long. A stranger seemed particularly anxious to get to close quarters with those who obstructed my path. The next day a report laid on my desk explained that the argument was started in order to "beat me up," while the solicitous stranger was none other than a Secret Service operator.

While present at the meeting, I demanded that the Central Labour Council either repudiate their name appearing on the circulars advertising the previous Sunday meeting, or explain how it came to be there. An officer of the Machinists' Union said that the meeting was arranged by them but that the speakers had been changed after the printing of the circular, and added that Anna Louise Strong had told him it would be all right to announce that the Central Labour Council was back of the meeting. The President of the council, Robert L. Proctor, denounced the use of the central body's name. At the same meeting, however, the same Central Labour Council endorsed a call for a mass meeting to be held the following Sunday afternoon, for the purpose of organizing a "Soldiers, Sailors, and Workmen's Council, or soviet!" When the thirteen men arrested for the Sunday riot were placed on trial, W. N. Stumpf, the man charged with assaulting Captain Searing, said: "Don't bother about a lawyer for me; the Defense Committee of the I.W.W. will furnish me an attorney."

We have seen how the organization of a soviet was planned in Seattle. It is well to call to the reader's mind that the radicals at the National Labour Congress in Chicago, on January sixteenth, demanded the organization of American Soviets. This was the congress called to consider a programme for liberating Thos. J. Mooney and Warren K. Billings, then serving life terms for murder in connection with bomb outrages committed in connection with a preparedness parade in San Francisco.

As stated by the *Post-Intelligencer* of January 17, 1919:

The climax at the Chicago convention was reached when a motion picture was shown of the Mooney case, one film showing American soldiers carrying an

American flag in the San Francisco preparedness parade, and there were hisses from many of the radicals when this was flashed on the screen.

A telegram was then read from Eugene V. Debs, addressed to E. B. Ault, who was in attendance at the meeting, which said in part:

The hour has struck for action. Long-winded resolutions and humble petitions to corporation tools in public office...are worse than useless. The convention can do no less than demand his (Mooney's) unconditional release and issue an ultimatum to that effect, giving due notice if that fails, a general strike will follow at a specified time and industry be paralyzed throughout the land.

One delegate shouted: "We'll make this country a desert like Arizona."

A message was also read from five members of the executive board of the I.W.W., pledging that organization to support a general strike.

Of course, Gompers and the American Federation of Labour were bitterly attacked. A telegram of greeting was also received from the Seattle "Soldiers, Sailors, and Workmen's Council," although it had had as yet no open meeting in Seattle, and its members consisted of the five ringleaders only!

On the same night, January sixteenth, a meeting of 5,000 I.W.W.'s was held at their favourite spot, Fourth Avenue and Virginia Street. A resolution was adopted, condemning all law-enforcing officials.

The *Post-Intelligencer* of the seventeenth had the following to say of this meeting:

Following the chairman, F. Clifford spoke. He told his hearers that the workers ought to take over, own, and run the machines of industry. He urged cooperation of the workers at the next election, told them to stick together at the polls, and if they then could not "get it by the ballot route, get it by the bullet route."

I was present during the entire meeting. As it broke up, 500 men took the lead and the crowd of 5,000 followed, starting toward the jail, half a mile away.

In speaking of the parade after the meeting, the *Post-Intelligencer* said:

Shouting defiance at the police, the leaders reached Jefferson Street and Third Avenue. (One block from police headquarters.) A few of them turned down Jefferson Street toward the waterfront. The others, however, kept on Yesler Way in the direction of the police station.

"Come on to the police station," urged the leaders. The others wavered, then obeyed.

At that instant those in the van saw a column of fourteen mounted policemen moving down the Yesler Way hill from the police station to meet them. Behind came four automobile trucks containing sixty policemen armed with carbines, followed by five squads of patrolmen on foot armed with night sticks...

For a space of several minutes the I.W.W. element followed their leaders in the "battle hymn" of the organization. The second stanza was barely started when the five squads of mounted policemen came down the street and sidewalks on both sides in a solid body. The crowd of singers was swept before them...Within five minutes after the police had started work, Yesler Way between Second and Third avenues was as bare of loitering crowds as on a Sunday at midnight.

On the same day, January sixteenth, that the Mooney Congress in Chicago was hissing the American flag, advocating a general strike and passing I.W.W. resolutions — with many of its members from the state of Washington, including "Jimmy" Duncan, and our good friend, E. B. Ault, who acted as secretary of the convention — members of the Central Labour Council in Seattle were encouraging, abetting, and protecting the Reds who met and marched down the street to take the city jail.

And on that same night an order was issued by the Metal Trades Council in Seattle, ordering a strike of 25,000 workmen employed in the shipyards, building government ships in Seattle alone, and requests were sent to the shipyard workers of the entire Pacific coast to take like action. Nothing could prove more conclusively that there was a widespread conspiracy throughout the Union for a concerted effort to establish bolshevism.

The men in the main did not understand what the leaders were doing. They were not permitted to vote as to whether they would strike or not. I talked with dozens of workmen from the yards, as did many of my friends, and outside of the leading agitators, none of them wanted to go on strike. *But when ordered to go on strike,, these men obeyed,* so thoroughly had they had it drilled into them the iniquity and perfidy of a man who would "scab."

In speaking of the manner in which the shipyard strike was called, the *Times* of January 17th said:

Disregarding appeals from some delegates that the workers themselves be given opportunity to express their views on the final question by a referendum ballot, fifty-seven delegates representing the Seattle Metal Trades Council last night voted to call a strike of the 25,500 members of the twenty-one affiliated unions next Tuesday morning at lo o'clock, provided the owners of shipyard and contract shops concerned do not in the meantime sign the council's blanket wage agreement.

On the same day, the Seattle *Union Record* printed a statement under great headlines: Shipyard Workers to Strike Tuesday, and another dispatch on the same page to the effect that the Tacoma Metal Trades Council had taken the same action. In the same issue a story was printed ridiculing Gompers's statement that "Bolshevism is a menace," and followed by a reproduction of the constitution of the Russian Soviet Republic, copied from the *Nation* of New York City. Preceding the constitution itself the *Record* says:

The *Nation*, New York City, of January fourth, has done a distinct service in printing in full the constitution of the Russian Socialist Federated Soviet Republic in its latest form as adopted July 10, 1918.

Editorially the *Record* comments on the publication of the constitution as follows:

So much misinformation has been spread about Bolshevism and the Russian Soviet Republic, that the *Union Record* takes pleasure in commending to its readers' notice the article printed in the last two columns of this page. It is worth careful reading by any one who is sincerely trying to understand what is going on in Russia.

Of course the *Record* demanded, as usual, the discharge of Chief of Police Warren, as a direct menace to the peace of the community and the recall of myself as mayor. In glaring headlines they also printed the resolution passed at the Mooney Congress, which demanded the destruction of the American Federation of Labour and the recall of Samuel Gompers as president of the Federation, with Mooney endorsed as a candidate for the position. Perhaps they were following a plan; perhaps they were preparing for future events — we shall see. We knew exactly what the plan was and we thought we knew what the result would be. There is a well-worn adage to the effect that if you give one rope enough he will hang himself.

As a result of the police interfering with their two previous street parades, the leaders by word of mouth and the *Union Record* through its columns claimed the "right of free speech" had been abridged. I therefore assisted in securing a hall where "free-speech" advocates could meet on the following Sunday. They did meet and followed their programme by openly forming the "Soldiers, Sailors, and Workmen's Council" which had been secretly planned some time before! It was now thought that with the shipyard workers out on strike and a general strike being agitated, the time was ripe for the public formation of a soviet. A. E. Miller was advertised as the chairman of the meeting, and when the great hall opened on Sunday, January nineteenth, more than 5,000 persons were present, the overflow crowd going up to their old meeting place at Fourth and Virginia streets. The meeting was conducted under the joint auspices of the Seattle Metal Trades Council and the Central Labour Council. A resolution was passed authorizing five delegates from every working-class organization in the city to meet at the Metal Trades Council on the following Saturday evening to perfect the organization of the "Soldiers, Sailors, and Workmen's Council." Frank A. Rust, manager of the Labour Temple Association, was one of the speakers. Mr. Rust is reputed to be a conservative labour leader and yet he, in the presence of my successor Mayor C. B. Fitzgerald, said to me: "I am not for revolution now. I am afraid it cannot win, but if I thought it could win, I would be for it down the line."

Again the hypocritical propaganda of aiding the returned soldiers was talked of in order to win their support for this revolutionary organization. The next day the streets were flooded with circulars headed: Chief of Police Warren Must Go, and closing with the statement:

Workers, go to your labour meetings and demand his removal in no uncertain terms. This loathsome character can be removed by you, the organized workers, through your economic power, if nothing else will prevail.

They knew I would never remove any man for doing his duty and they could have struck until the cows came home; Warren would not have been "fired" to please them or any one else. It is hard enough to get a man that will do his duty fearlessly, and the more law breakers "knock" such a man, the greater the proof of his well doing. "No thief ever felt the halter draw with good opinion of the law."

Agitation was increased. Men worked but little in the shipyards, but gathered in knots to listen to the revolutionists, and on January twenty-first, at 10 a. m., *all the shipyard workers in Seattle went out on strike. And the fight was on between the Government and the workers.*

The lowest wage paid for common labour in the shipyards was $4.16 and the loudly vaunted reason of the strike was to aid the men who received this minimum wage. As a matter of fact, there were but few men in the shipyards who received this small amount. At the Skinner & Eddy plant (the largest in the city) only six men out of a total of 14,629 received this minimum wage The following statement, taken from the books of the Skinner & Eddy Corporation, show conclusively that the strike was not called to increase the wages of the $4.16 men:

NUMBER OF MEN	DAILY WAGE
6	$4.16
81	4.48
3,713	4.64
571	4.64 to $5.00
6,064	5.00 to 6.00
2,911	6.00 to 7.00
568	7.00 to 8.00
815	8.00 and up

In the neighbouring city of Tacoma 15,000 workers walked out.

The propaganda regarding the soldiers and sailors joining the ranks of the I.W.W. had been spread so broadcast throughout the country that on January twenty-second Senator Johnson of California stated on the floor of" the Senate that "press dispatches claimed that after dispersing a demonstration of I.W. W.'s in Seattle it was found that among the outcast I.W.W.'s were soldiers of the United States who were being fed by the I.W.W. and who were without resources or money or food." Our senator from Washington, Wesley L. Jones, wired to Harold Preston, then chairman of our County Council of Defence, and myself as mayor, requesting information in relation to this matter. I replied, as did Mr. Preston, that it was untrue; that no soldiers or sailors had been arrested charged with being law violators; that no soldier or sailor outcasts were being fed by the I.W.W.; that so far as I knew they were with the authorities for the enforcement of law to the man; that all employers had opened places for them upon their return; that there was no unemployment in the city, and that up to the day of the strike labour was in good demand.

But from house to house, at night, went the Red agitators, preaching discontent and hatred of our Government, and *within twenty-four hours of the declaration of the shipyard strike,* open agitation began for the calling of a *general strike.* On the night of January twenty-second, thirty-six hours after the shipyard workers struck, a meeting was held at the Central Labour Council, and at this meeting a resolution was passed, asking every union in Seattle to go on a general strike in support of the workers in the shipyard industries. In describing the meeting, the *Union Record,* under the caption "General Strike to Be Voted Upon by Unions," said:

With cheers for the solidarity of Labour, and without a dissenting vote [an untruth], the Central Labour Council last night resolved to ask every union to go on a general strike in support of the workers in the shipyard industry...As explained by Chairman A. E. Miller of the Metal Trades Strike Committee, Business Agent Von Carnop, Delegate Jack Mullane, and others, the plan is for "*mass action* and *mass results.*" Hulet M. Wells said when he took the platform: "Seattle is one place where a universal strike can be pulled off with success..."

Concluding the debate, Delegate Fred Nelson unfurled one of the big coloured posters, showing a soldier and a sailor in uniform, and a worker in overalls, with the motto: "Together We Win," amidst a storm of applause which lasted several minutes.

"That's the way I came back from Chicago," shouted Delegate King who had just returned from the Mooney Congress, "sleeping between soldiers and sailors, and they are all with us."

Thus the stage was set. The next day members of the 346th Field Artillery returned to Seattle. I wondered at the time whether the revolutionists really believed they could make bolshevists of these loyal heroes. Before me is a report stating that they did expect and plan to absorb these soldiers. The thousands of returned soldiers gathered at the Hippodrome to be welcomed — the same hall which but a few hours before had been filled with men who aimed to destroy the Government these men had fought to save.

As mayor, I was requested to make a short address. It was hard to stand before those men and not tell them in plain words just what was to be attempted, but doing so would only have postponed the crisis. I knew it had to come and did not want to put it off. We were ready.

I said in speaking of the Reds:

To that minority who would rule or overthrow this Government, I say, "Beware." Passion, noise, declamation, disorder, riot, treason, sedition, anarchy, are but the bubbles floating on the surface of the great river. The depths flow silently on to the sea bearing on their bosom the hopes and ideals of all humanity, pregnant with unknown and unthought possibilities of happiness and peace for all. Our country has been the beacon light for all the peoples of the world. Let us stand for orderly, well-thought-out progress; let us construct, not destroy; let us

29

stand for order, not disorder; let us stand by our flag in this crucial time and when the smoke and dust and noise have passed away, our children and our children's children will reap the great reward.   God Bless You and Keep You Safe.

Chapter Three - The Labour Situation in Seattle and Throughout the Northwest Preceding the Attempted Revolution

Before proceeding to tell the story of the general strike or attempted revolution in Seattle I want to give the reader a little idea of some of the events which had immediately preceded and led up to this ominous labour situation throughout the Northwest and especially in Seattle.

The Convention of the Industrial Workers of the World in Chicago, in 1914, took an open stand against our Government. The result of this action was soon apparent in the West, and in and around Seattle, open denunciation of the Government becoming the order of the day. The street corners of Seattle and adjoining "towns and villages" became the nightly forum for the soapboxers and little or no attempt was made to enforce the law *prohibiting street meetings which caused obstruction of traffic.* No effort whatever, so far as we know, was made by the authorities to punish the open teaching of sedition. Sabotage, too, came into as general use as was consistent with safety and the preaching thereof became as free and untrammeled as the preaching of the Gospel.

Soon stickers appeared in the camps explaining how to destroy or injure machinery; accidents to logging and milling machinery became of daily occurrence, and almost every bunk house became a debating club where the best methods of practising sabotage, *with safety,* were freely discussed. The output was decreased and men did but a part of a day's work, grudging every movement put forth that meant production. Strike after strike occurred, almost any excuse sufficing as a reason Impossible demands were made, the best of food was refused as uneatable, and a black pall of trouble settled over practically the entire Northwest.

Apples were bruised in the packing so they would decay in but a short time. Logging engines were turned loose down the mountain sides, and fires became daily more numerous. Police officers, soldiers, sailors, and all forces charged with enforcement of law were openly denounced and abused If one I.W.W. was arrested, hundreds more came from the surrounding country and tried to overcrowd the jails, laughed and sang, kept everyone awake, and generally kept things in a state of turmoil. There was absolutely no respect for duly-constituted authority, for law and order. Like the noisy frogs, the I.W.W. apparently believed that noise spelled numbers, force, and power to control.

Everett, a city of 30,000 and but thirty miles from Seattle, finally passed a law prohibiting the obstruction of traffic by means of street meetings, and a strong effort was made to enforce it. The I.W.W. were equally determined that this law should not be enforced, and continued their attempts to hold nightly meetings in the down-town section. In desperation, Everett's outraged citizens organized to protect their city and drove certain I.W.W.'s from their midst, several being tarred and feathered. They were given to understand, in no uncertain language, that Everett was through with the I.W.W. for all time.

Bent upon revenge, the I.W.W.'s met in Seattle, armed themselves, chartered a steamboat, and sailed for Everett to enforce the "right of free speech." They were met at the wharf by an armed group of men led by the sheriff and refused a landing. Someone opened fire, either from the boat or from the land; the testimony to this day is conflicting as to who fired the first shot. A battle ensued. Several were killed on both sides, but the boat finally departed and came back to our city, carrying with it the wounded and the dead, and leaving several of Everett's citizens sleeping their last sleep. Wholesale arrests were made upon the boat's arrival in Seattle. A trial was had, both sides presenting directly conflicting stories. No one was found guilty, but to this day Everett has had no further open and violent disorder.

As a result of the Everett trouble, thousands of converts of I.W.W.'ism hurried to the centres of population; Seattle, as the largest city in the Northwest, getting her full quota. For a time things looked bad, but no open revolt took place. There did come, however, a sharp division in the population, the vast majority, of course, demanding enforcement of existing laws. The city government, as then constituted, refused. Public sentiment became so crystallized against the then mayor that there was talk of his recall. A former mayor had built a stand in a down-town park for the convenience of the I.W.W., but they almost invariably refused to use it. What they wanted was to be put in jail, to agitate and become martyrs. They did not want free speech — they wanted free board and free advertising.

Conditions in the lumber industry became worse daily. Men could not be secured to do the work and, when secured, would not work. In the lumber camps of Oregon and Washington there were at least 40,000 I.W.W.'s.

With this country drawing nearer, daily, to the world war raging in Europe, Councilman Allan Dale thought it but proper that the city government should be the first to set an example of respect for *our flag*. He introduced, and had passed by the City Council, a resolution providing that at the opening of each session the council clerk should carry the flag into the chamber, whereupon each member was to salute and stand at attention until the flag was in its standard beside the president's desk. One member of the council, Oliver T. Erickson, voted against the resolution. Erickson also absented himself from the opening ceremony, and never thereafter saluted our flag when it was carried into the council chamber. A fine commentary on the patriotism and loyalty of a man who owes all that he has to our country — and Erickson was born in Minnesota, *not in Europe.*

Up at the Central Labour Council certain delegates openly fought the Government, and our flag was refused a place over their building. Finally, Frank W. Gates, a labour union man who was a member of the King County Council of Defence, a patriot whose three sons went to war, climbed the flag pole and nailed the Stars and Stripes to the mast. Mr. Gates made the following signed statement:

Ten days before war was declared the United States flag which had flown over the Labour Temple disappeared. The Central Labour Council met that night. I was a delegate representing the Painters and Decorators' Local 300. I made a motion that a new flag be purchased, but no action was taken.

The following Wednesday I wanted to know why the flag had not been raised over the Labour Temple, and James Duncan in his office told me that the reason was that "our flag was an emblem of war and bloodshed and that if it was raised the red flag must be hung beside it!" I told him that if Labour did not put the flag up the patriotic citizens of Seattle would do so and that this would put Labour in a bad light. If war was declared and the labour officials did not fly the American flag, I said I would, with the help of loyal labour people, raise the flag myself. He said if I did, "the red flag would fly with it." I said: "The people will take care of the red flag."

That same night I fought on the floor to get the flag up, but James Duncan led the opposition to it, and the motion was tabled and laid over. The Spanish War veterans called me up that night and said, "If Labour does not fly the flag over the Temple, we will put it up ourselves."

Again I went to the labour officials and asked: "Why is not the flag on our Temple?" Duncan said: "I don't know as it ever will fly from this temple." I then asked Bob Hesketh, who was a member of the Finance Committee, if he would vote with me and back me up if I used labour funds to buy the flag. He said, "Yes." I wanted the flag to be bought with Labour's money. I then went to the Labour Temple and called on patriotic labour men to come with me and buy the flag. At least twenty men responded, and we bought the flag and we went up to the Labour Temple, and with an impromptu ceremony, hung the flag. The following Monday the officials became so alarmed at the public sentiment that they pulled down the flag I had paid for and purchased another and hung it in its place and returned mine to me. I stood the cost of the first flag myself. The flag has never been taken down, and it won't be either.

Immediately upon our country declaring war every effort was made by the I.W.W. and radical elements to obstruct the success of our Government. Hulet M. Wells, together with others of his stripe, conspired to resist and obstruct the Selective Draft Act. Anna Louise Strong at once became an open, *Red Revolutionist,* and one of Wells's chief co-workers. Sam Sadler, another well-known I.W.W. already referred to, became a leader with Wells in his effort to stop the selective service draft. So openly defiant did Wells and Sadler become that they were finally arrested, tried, and convicted, and are at this writing serving their sentences in the Federal prison. Miss Strong was one of the principal witnesses at their trial.

On April seventh, the day after this country declared war, a great mass meeting was called at the Arena, Seattle's largest auditorium, with a seating capacity of 8,000 for the purpose of declaring Seattle's intention of supporting the Government and to unify all loyal elements under one head. The situation was critical. It was a time for unity of action — not for division. The loyalists invited the following speakers to address the assemblage: President Henry Suzzalo of the University of Washington; Rev. Carter Helm Jones, one of the leading ministers of the city; Judge Thomas Burke, famous lawyer and leading citizen and loyal every ounce, and myself. Robert C. Saunders, now U.S. District Attorney, who subsequently sent three of his sons to the front, was chairman.

The doors were opened to a crowd which overflowed the building. The opening song was sung; the people, stern, white faced, determined, sang the chorus. There was no laughter or smiling. It was stern business and the crowd meant business. The chairman introduced the Reverend Mr. Jones first. Jones was inspired. He made a speech that lifted the very souls of men to Heaven — his love of country rang in every sentence, every syllable, every word! He spoke of France, of Belgium, of its murdered; he demanded the defeat of Germany and all her policies. It was immense! I could feel my heart pound. My blood raced like a torrent in my veins. Everybody felt the same. He sat down. The crowd arose and cheered itself hoarse. It was the greatest speech any of us had ever heard. I would cross the ocean to hear such another.

I was next called and did my best, taking as my main topic the Selective Service Act. I praised it "as the most democratic method of selecting a country's defenders ever devised." I said: "If it is a duty, alt should share it; if a privilege, all should enjoy it." I denounced the camouflaged traitors who were obstructing our Government, and impressed on the multitude that it was not a rich man's war, nor a poor man's war, but was a war for all of us, by all of us, with equal sacrifice for all. When I closed by saying, "We are embarking upon a path that will be wet with tears and stained with blood, but we must and will follow it to the end," the audience arose and sang "The Star-Spangled Banner."

Then came Doctor Suzzalo, who delivered a most wonderful address, brimful of hope, love, and patriotic fervour, and again the great crowd responded. Then Judge Burke, about five feet high and more than seventy years old, took the platform. The judge, besides being a great orator, is one of the clearest thinkers in our country, one of our most able and patriotic citizens, and is a real loo-per-cent. American! He told of the cruelty of Germany; he recited the rape of Belgium and the murder of our own people. As he talked the faces of his hearers became dark and grim; hard lines appeared. There was not much applause Feeling was too intense. But when he finished, the hopes of the Anna Louise Strongs, the Sam Sadlers, the Hulet Wells's, and all anti-war fac-

33

tions in Seattle, had vanished. Every man and woman of the 8,000 stood ready to do their duty *no matter what happened. Seattle was united.*

In reality, Seattle was and always has been loyal, but a few loud-mouthed traitors had actually succeeded in creating the impression that this was not so. That meeting settled the question for the entire war. I went home but did not sleep very much. The longer I thought about it, the more I felt that hanging by the neck was too good for any one who was false to our flag and our country. I am very proud that I was privileged to take part in this great demonstration. I feel that it did Seattle and our country good. I know it did me good. I knew then that when the time of trouble came, when anarchy lined the sky, Seattle with her best and bravest would meet the crisis and stand four square.

Then came the establishment of shipyards in our midst. Seattle was beginning to build ships; the waterfront soon took strange shape, and from every part of the country came an influx of strangers. More yards and still more yards were established, but with the coming of strangers came also a change in labour and civic affairs. The Government needed men to build ships, and in order to secure them, gave practical exemption from military service to those who entered the yards. Loggers quit the camps, coal miners quit the mines, and many structural iron workers who had "trained" with the McNamaras found profitable employment. Boys who wanted to escape the draft joined the working forces, but the majority went to the shipyards in much the same spirit as did the boys who went to war — as a necessary patriotic duty to their country. Soon the 15,000 industrial workers increased to 65,000, and as the yards came into being under closed-shop conditions, the Government continued them as such. Thus there came to be in Seattle a union membership of more than 60,000.

Here in the Northwest stood the biggest body of spruce in the country — timber that was better suited for airplanes than any other. The Government immediately tried to secure this spruce for its war work through the existing lumber camps and mills, but at every turn found the I.W.W. blocking its path! Every nerve was exerted by the I.W.W.'s to render the Government helpless! It became necessary for the Government to establish its own camps in the undeveloped forests and, through regulation and supervision, drive the I.W.W.'s from the existing ones, and produce spruce to help win the war.

Mr. Donovan, of the Bloedel-Donovan Mill Company of Bellingham, Wash., in testifying before the Congressional Investigating Committee on August 23, 1919, in Seattle, on I.W.W. efforts to obstruct the Government's spruce work, said:

As soon as war started, the I.W.W. became very active in the woods. I do not know whether there was any connection between that organization and German agents. We met their opposition, which was manifested by driving spikes in logs, blowing up logging engines, starting fires in the woods, and anything else that would delay production.

Our company had one very bad fire that the I.W.W. set. We had an engine blown up and a man killed, though I cannot be sure that the I.W.W. did this. We found an average of one spike a week in the logs at the mill, whereas usually we found one in six months or one a year. One ship that sailed from Bellingham with lumber was reported on fire at sea from the result of a fire bomb set aboard before she sailed.

Not more than 20 per cent, of the men employed were engaged in such activities; the other 80 per cent, were loyal and earnest. When the loyal legion was formed, nearly all the loggers and millmen in the Northwest, including Oregon, Washington, and part of Idaho, joined. From that time on we had no trouble.

In every camp the effort was made to eradicate the I.W.W.'s, and when driven from the woods they found ready employment in the cities — many of them in the shipyards. In all the previous history of the I.W.W. movement, it had planned to destroy from the outside the American Federation of Labour. But upon the outbreak of war the I.W.W.'s, forced to join the unions or go without work, began to "bore from within," their aim being to take possession of the already functioning labour unions. Prominent members of the organization have told me that this was the result of plans made in Petrograd by Lenin and his crowd.

When Lenin and Trotsky decided that their government must fall if our Government did not, they sent their agents to these shores to overthrow our Government, and upon their arrival in Seattle, they found the I.W.W. already in existence and functioning along bolshevist lines. They, therefore, joined the organization, supported it with their funds, and *led the fight against our Government by using the already-at-hand organization.*

The old trade unions of Seattle were progressive but not revolutionary. Their organizations were the result of years of effort, toil, and struggle. They knew that revolution was not the true route. They believed in gradual evolution and never-ceasing progress, but now a new note began to be sounded. A few of the old leaders were syndicalists at heart, while the new ones, clever, forceful, determined, gradually overthrew the more conservative leaders and took their places. Meetings that used to adjourn at twelve midnight now were prolonged until almost dawn. The Reds knew what they were doing and what they wanted. When the home owner and family man was forced to go home, they remained and toward morning did exactly as they pleased. The passage of revolutionary resolutions became more and more frequent. Labour was getting a bad name. At eleven p. m. the meeting would be American; at midnight it would be fifty fifty, while at two in the morning, only the Reds remained, with sometimes a few so-called conservative leaders who were *too cowardly to raise their voices in defence of their country.* Most of these leaders, who denounced bolshevism and I.W.W.'ism in private, were afraid to do so in public, fearing *they would lose the paltry jobs they held as officers of their unions, as secretaries, walking delegates, etc.* It was by pursuing these methods that the radicals finally succeeded in securing control of the Central

Labour Council of Seattle, which is composed of representatives of all the unions in the city, and still contains many loyal men; who, through weakness and lack of fighting spirit, have allowed a militant "bummery" to control their affairs. This, then, was the condition of Seattle's affairs in 1917.

Chapter Four - The New American Revolution Planned and Developed while They Sleep

And now along the war-worn land
A mass would raise a blood-red lie
To flaunt across the restless sky
And call it FLAG — and some have planned
To rule our sacred state
With lust and death and hate.
White crosses gleam upon the hill
Of every Flanders town, but still
Some forget the holy sleep
Of Men who died to keep
Them Free.

— Leo H. Lassen, in the *Seattle Star.*

IN THE western suburbs of Portland, Oregon, there is a little village called Linnton. This village came into being during boom time and buildings were built which oft-times have since stood empty. One of these buildings had been used in the palmy days as a pool and billiard hall. It was now deserted.

On the night of October 22, 1918, a strange body of men gathered within its walls; men who were strangers to Linnton; men who did not live in Portland, or Oregon; men who were called together from far-away places, for a definite purpose, a purpose which could be carried out only in secrecy and darkness. One by one they crept into the old building, presented their credentials, and then sat in silence until all the elect were accounted for. The village slept, and probably until this page is read not one man or woman in the little hamlet has ever heard of this fateful gathering, and yet these strange men, with turned-up coat collars, with hats pulled down over their eyes, had met to destroy that which is most dear to the people of Linnton and to the liberty-loving folks of all the world.

Nearly half a hundred people attended. They came from all over the United States; one from faraway Siberia, one from each of twenty-seven states of this Union, and one, the most important, came with credentials and a message from the Soviet Government of Russia. Every man was carefully examined and vouched for before he was admitted. Each had certain credentials. One would have thought it was a meeting of some secret society at war with civilization, and it was! Representatives attended from Lynn, Mass., from Butte, Mont., from Houston, Tex., and from Paterson, N. J.

The man from Russia read his instructions and his letter. Short, quiet comments were made. These men were not talkers; they were doers of deeds, and such deeds! Each man reported as to conditions in his own locality. All seemed to know that the World War was nearing its end. All expected chaos to follow. All, everyone, was for revolution; the only questions considered were: "When? Where? How?"

The meeting finally decided:

That the time is ripe for the *overthrow of our Government - ripe for the establishment in its place of a soviet government similar to the one in operation in Russia;*

That the Government should be overthrown by peaceable means if possible; but that if resistance was encountered, *force and violence of whatever character necessary should be used;*

That the lumber woods of Washington had the best-organized band of revolutionists in the United States; that the beginning must be made where these men could help;

That a shipyard strike in Seattle, therefore, was the logical place to start;

That the Macy award was to be the excuse;

That the Macy *Government* Board was to be the target; and

That *a general strike in Seattle should immediately follow the shipyard strike, which would be spread to many different localities, finally resulting in the overthrow of our Government and the placing in power, as dictators, some of the very men present.*

The unanimous agreement of all present as to the feasibility and certain success of the plan ended the business before the meeting. The scenario was finished; the meeting adjourned; one by one the conspirators left the building; one by one they left Portland, soon to reappear in their respective communities and carry out their respective roles. However, there were men present who had other credentials than those which admitted them. These men represented society, you and me. Unknown to each other, they were there. Before morning the right people knew about the meeting, its plans, its decisions.

Within three days events took place in widely scattered sections of this country showing that the work had begun. Every move ran true to schedule. There was no delay, no red tape. The work was admirably done. Strike after strike was called all over the country. The colonization in the shipyards went on smoothly. The aliens, the revolutionists, the I.W.W.'s came from everywhere. Plausible, forceful talkers, it was not hard for them to spread discontent. Any one who wanted work could get it. The propagandists infected one shift one week and the next week quit and worked with another crew. Literally tons of literature were distributed; thousands of agitators redoubled their efforts in the woods, in the shops, in the yards, on the streets, in the lodging houses, everywhere. Never did a political party carry on such a campaign. Bearded aliens whose faces had never known a razor visited their countrymen at night. The Russian bolsheviki would tell their prospects: "This fight here is our fight in Russia. With capitalism surviving in America, Russia will again go back to Czarism. By helping here and *being ready,* we help Lenin and all Russian patriots." This is taken verbatim from a report of Secret Service men.

Several who attended the Linnton meeting came to Seattle. They took part in all the revolutionary agitation up to and including the general strike. Money seemed to be very plentiful with the agitators. Never was one arrested who did not have plenty of funds; just as soon as he was booked, the I.W.W. defence attorney — an American born, educated in our schools and colleges, at our expense — would appear and make the fight for his release.

A post office for I. W.W.'s and "Reds" was opened in a book store on First Avenue. The volume of mail was so great that it required an extra clerk to distribute it. One I.W.W. organizer walked into the clubhouse of the Elks, one of our most patriotic orders, applied for membership, and received his mail with checks, subscriptions, and I.W.W. literature for quite a long time at the Elks' business office. One day a man of the same name opened a letter by mistake and was amazed to find post office orders for a considerable sum with many applications for I.W.W. membership from Pasco, Washington, a railroad division point. Of course the I.W.W. never became, a member, and his use of the Elks' club ended right there. In order to get the workers to read the literature, which came principally from a Chicago publisher. Jack London and other prominent authors' names were printed on the cover as authors, despite the fact that the pamphlet itself contained references to occurrences which happened long after London died. This made no difference, circulation was thus secured, converts were made, and many contented workmen became "class conscious," grew to hate the employer, the Government, and everyone else.

Such is the power of the printed word. Society never has as yet sensed the value of advertising ideas, and perhaps never will until it is too late. The revolutionist always has understood it. A merchant will advertise the merits of his goods but *never the greatness and goodness of his government.* Usually when he talks about it, he does as you and I do, and talks about *the little holes in the fabric but seldom explains how the little faults can be easily mended by the people themselves.*

If the Portland meeting had been exposed it would merely have saved the agitators the necessity of advertising. The smug citizen would have grinned and gone about his work as usual. Every agitator in the world would have known of the plan and its fruition would not have been checked. If one knows what his opponent is going to do, one can prepare to meet the situation. Surprise is always on the side of the attacker unless the attacked is forewarned. I felt that the quicker things came to a head the better for the country. If it was to happen, I wanted it to happen in Seattle, their chosen battle ground. If they lost here they would lose everywhere. We were sure of our police force, sure of the U.S. District Attorney, sure of our chief of police, and *sure of our returned soldiers.* I was also sure that the workers, union and non-union, would align themselves with their country when they understood the perfidy of their leaders. I never talked with any man or woman about the Linnton plan until long after the general strike was over. The most silent individuals sometimes tell the most important things to very dear friends who retell them to others. The talkative man seldom talks about the things he should keep secret. Very often many words are a very useful smoke screen.

We have seen how the Mooney Congress in Chicago, the shipyard strike in Seattle, the agitation for the general strike, the troubles in the lumber woods, the formation of the Soldiers, Sailors, and Workmen's Soviet, the articles in the *Record,* etc., all seemed to fit in beautifully with some general plan. The thought probably came unprompted to the reader: Can such things just happen? Can so many different, isolated occurrences be brought about at the right time, in the right place, without a plan? The answer is. No. The Mooney Congress, the nation-wide agitation, the tons of propaganda, the colonization of Seattle, the lumber workers' sabotage, the formation of the Soviets, the shipyard strike, the immediate successful agitation for a general strike did not just happen or come out of the thin air of coincidence.

The Linnton meeting and the plans laid there brought these matters about. The plan was carefully laid by shrewd men, men who had brains to conspire and courage to execute; men who hated our Government, hated all governments except the Lenin autocracy in Russia. These men had unbounded means, secret support in high places, and but for fortuitous circumstances and Seattle's loyalty might have changed the history of our country, for a time at least. A great deal of blood would have been shed, innocent blood in the main; a fire would have started which, gaining headway, would have been mighty hard to check, but *Seattle was loyal* and true and met the issue without flinching. Seattle's citizenship stood by our flag and the country was the gainer.

We have seen how the shipyard workers struck; how their delegations went to other cities to agitate and call out their brethren; how the Soviets were formed, and how *at once the general strike was agitated and started on its fateful way.* The Seattle *Union Record* spilled more red ink daily, the unrest increased, the name of Piez of the Shipping Board became anathema, the slaughter of Chief Warren was planned, and it looked as though Hell would soon break loose. The Soldiers, Sailors, and Workmen's Council, formed ostensibly to take care of returning soldiers and sailors, as a matter of fact, was formed for the purpose of taking over all governmental authority during and after the strike. Five delegates were decided upon from each working-class organization, each organization was to conduct its industrial affairs, but the Soldiers, Sailors, and Workmen's Council (Soviet) was to possess supreme authority. Much ado was made over bills pending before the Legislature for the relief of soldiers. As a matter of fact, no place in the United States provided better for the returning soldiers than did the city of Seattle; several organizations kept open house and all soldiers were able to secure remunerative employment. The state of Washington appropriated $500,000 to be used for relief purposes. In the hope, however, of capturing returning soldiers and sailors, and turning them into revolutionists, every device was used to win their favour. A large fund was raised, contributed by different labour bodies few of whose members knew of any other plan than to help the returning soldiers and sailors.

On January twenty-fifth a meeting was held by the Soldiers, Sailors, and Workmen's Council at the hall of the Metal Trades Council. At this meeting, during the course of discussion, one Russian Bolshevist came to the platform and, among other things, said:

In 1905 the Russian sailors proved what they could do, and blood ran red. Again, on several occasions, blood ran to prove that they were always true to the cause. In Petrograd the sailors again proved it, and this city ran with blood. The sailors of Bremerton (meaning Puget Sound Naval Station) will be on hand when needed, and the streets of Seattle will run red with blood and the Soldiers, Sailors, and Workmen's Council need not worry but what they (the sailors) will do their part. (Cheers.)

This is an actual quotation from a report of the meeting by an operative of the Department of Justice at Washington.

At a later meeting held at Painters' Hall, a constitution was ordered prepared, which was to supplant the Constitution of the United States. At a subsequent meeting, held at 310 Collins Building, in accordance with a report made by the Minute Men, it was agreed that the Soldiers, Sailors, and Workmen's Council "was to be a delegate body, representing the revolutionary spirit of the country, and that this delegate body was to be the future government of the country and in time — of the whole world!...That the delegates would not represent a false structure, but would have actual membership behind it, so that when called to act in the revolution they could depend on what they really had...That it would be the government of the country; that each organization was to be represented by their delegates; that it was identical with the Russian movement, and that they would take over and run all industries; that they would not compensate the capitalists for the industries at all, but just take them over."

A former janitor of one of our public schools who had been for years the "ad" writer and propaganda distributer for the man who "pulled teeth by day and practised law by night," was one of the leading delegates.

The constitution adopted was a cross between the Soviet Constitution of Russia and the I.W.W. Declaration of Principles. I quote now from the

Declaration of Principles of the Workers, Soldiers, and Sailors' Council

preceding the Constitution itself:

Society is divided into two classes, the working class and the employing class...We recognize the imperative necessity of developing working-class institutions to supersede those of the ruling class. We hail with admiration and pride the Russian revolution...We pledge ourselves to leave no stone unturned till the complete emancipation of the working class is an accomplished fact. The purpose of the Council of Workers, Soldiers, and Sailors is to organize all members of the working class into one organization and train them in the principles of mass action, in order that we may realize that accumulation of energy, that concentration of force, and continuity of resistance necessary to strike the final blow against capitalism. With these objects in view, we call upon all those who toil, regardless of race, creed, colour or sex, to rally to the standard of real democracy to bring about the *dictatorship* of the only useful class in society — the working class.

On January twenty-fifth, four days after the shipyard strike had been called, Seattle shipbuilders received the following telegrams from Mr. Charles Piez, director-general, United States Shipping Board, Emergency Fleet Corporation, and Mr. V. Everit Macy, chairman of the Labour Adjustment Board:

The Fleet Corporation feels that the men in your district have had every opportunity for a proper and fair hearing; that the men in striking violated the spirit and letter of their agreement with the Government; that they were in the highest degree unwise in the face of a falling market to stop work; and that, if they were successful in securing their demands by this means, the future of the entire shipbuilding industry in your district would be jeopardized.

The Fleet Corporation stands by the Macy Board decision and will do nothing more.

I ask you to make no efforts to resume operations unless the men are willing to accept the Labour Adjustment Board's decision. The Government is not so badly in need of ships that it will compromise on a question of principle.

(*Signed*) Piez.

Board regards going out of men in Puget Sound yards violation of agreement. Shipbuilding Labour Adjustment Board cannot countenance their action in any way.

(*Signed*) Macy.

The shipbuilders printed the above telegrams in the *Times* of January twenty-sixth, and accompanied them with this statement:

In connection with these telegrams it should be realized that the agreement referred to is that there should be no lockouts or strikes until peace is declared as evidenced by proclamation of the President. Our employees, and the public as well, must understand that we are now confronted with the absolute fact that the men must either return to work under the Macy award, or that shipbuilding with its commensurate payroll ceased in this community forever last Tuesday.

Skinner & Eddy Corporation,
J. F. Duthie & Co.,

Ames Shipbuilding & Drydock Company,
Todd Shipbuilding & Drydock Corporation,
Seattle North Pacific Shipbuilding Company.

These telegrams, however, had no effect whatsoever upon the strikers. Every hour brought reports of some union voting in favour of the general strike. As a matter of fact, not more than 10 per cent, of the workers in Seattle ever voted for the general strike. Each meeting was either packed with radicals before the conservative element arrived, or only the radicals were notified of the meeting.

All this time we were busy at the City Hall. The influenza epidemic seemed to be gaining. In the Legislature, the person who had collected $1,100 from the quarantined victims was busily engaged in lobbying and making open attacks against the city government. We were also doing everything possible to induce the Legislature to pass a great "land-reclamation bill" so that those of the returning soldiers and sailors who desired to secure for themselves a tract of irrigated land could do so on long-time and easy payments. But with all these added burdens, we did not slacken our preparations to meet the general strike, which now seemed certain to occur. We literally worked night and day.

In checking up the stocks of the various sporting-goods' stores, hardware stores, and pawnshops, in neighbouring cities as well as in Seattle, we discovered that more rifles, revolvers, and cartridges had been sold during the previous two weeks than during the past six months. At our request the merchants removed their stock of arms and ammunition from their shelves and all further open sales stopped. The efforts of the Metal Trades Council to tie up the entire shipbuilding industry of the United States and Canada continued unabated, their Conference Committee sending out hundreds of telegrams and letters throughout the United States calling for a general cessation of work in all shipyards. It is worthy of note also that on January twenty-eighth, in London, England, 200,000 men struck in the shipyards and other industries.

The general chorus of discontent was of course joined by the *Union Record* and this sheet on January twenty-fourth, under the headlines: "Boys Cheer in Passing Strike Headquarters," told of returning soldiers loudly cheering a large coloured poster showing a soldier, a sailor, and a worker arm in arm, with the motto: "Together We Win." Without giving the name of the soldier, the *Record* then quotes one of the men as saying:

Most of the soldiers who had come from the cities would be eager to join the Soldiers, Sailors, and Workmen's Council as soon as they were discharged from the service. Discontent with the old order of things and radical ideas are growing like wildfire in the army.

To keep the general-strike agitation at the fever stage, the boiler-makers held a mass meeting at the Hippodrome on Sunday, January twenty-sixth.

Talks were made on the general-strike votes being then taken by several unions; reports were received from delegates who had attended the Mooney Congress in Chicago; speeches were made in defence of the *Union Record;* the shipyard strike was gone over once more to keep up the spirit of the strikers, but in fact the meeting was for the purpose of showing "solidarity," to be used as a "club" to intimidate those unions that were "faltering" and failing to show a "solid front" in favour of the general strike. The *Union Record* quotes John McKelvey as saying during the course of his speech:

And now Piez says if we don't give in and go back to work, so these millionaires can go back to making their millions, they'll take the contracts away from Puget Sound, and do all the shipbuilding back East. Well, let 'em do it. If they want to start a revolution, let 'em start it.

Commenting editorially on the Piez and Macy telegrams, the *Record* on the same page says:

What ships have been built in the recent emergency were built *in spite* of the caveman findings of the Macy Board and not because of them.

Verily, the pot was boiling; was soon to boil over!

So far-reaching had been the plans laid by the leaders of the strike to stop all shipbuilding on the continent that on January twenty-eighth, at Victoria, B. C, the Victoria Metal Trades Council refused to assist in the repairs to the steamer *Admiral Watson,* the strikers saying: "We have received orders from the Seattle Metal Trades Council."

On the same day the Metal Trades Council held its regular meeting and promised to stand by all unions that came out in the sympathy strike and to communicate with all shipbuilding districts in the United States and Canada in order to effect a complete tie-up of all shipbuilding on the continent.

Having worked the workers up to the point where nothing seemingly remained but to set the date when the mass strike was to begin, 300 delegates, representing 110 of the 130 unions in Seattle, met on Sunday, February second, in an all-day session at the Labour Temple, and fixed the date for the general strike for 10 o'clock on the morning of Thursday, February sixth. All newspaper accounts of the meeting agree that the vote was "unanimous." Probably it was, because the "Conservatives" had been so terrified by the "Reds" that they dared not oppose them. In any event, this meeting was so "secret" that even the president of the Central Labour Council — who was not a delegate — was unable to gain admittance for three hours after the meeting had begun its session. At this meeting an "executive committee" was named to formulate ways and means of conducting the strike, as was also a "committee on tactics," to work in conjunction with a committee of the Metal Trades Council to send out notices to all local unions regarding the general strike; also to work out plans to extend the strike to other localities, and to be in readiness to be dispatched to any place where the general committee might deem it expedient to carry on this work.

It would be impossible to reproduce the many circulars and hand-bills which were thrown about the city at night to fan the flames of discontent, but one in particular I wish you to read which is reproduced herewith, verbatim. These hand-bills were being passed out in front of the Labour Temple on the night of February fourth, thirty-six hours before the strike.

Russia Did It

Shipyard Workers —You left the shipyards to enforce your demands for higher wages. Without you your employers are helpless. Without you they cannot make one cent of profit — their whole system of robbery has collapsed.

The shipyards are idle; the toilers have withdrawn even though the owners of the yards are still there. Are your masters building ships? No. Without your labour power it would take all the shipyard employers of Seattle and Tacoma working eight hours a day the next thousand years to turn out one ship. Of what use are they in the shipyards?

It is you and you alone who build the ships; you create all the wealth of society to-day; you make possible the $75,000 sable coats for millionaires' wives. It is you alone who can build the ships.

They can't build the ships. You can. Why don't you?

There are the shipyards; more ships are urgently needed; you alone can build them. If the masters continue their dog-in-the-manger attitude, not able to build the ships themselves and not allowing the workers to, there is only one thing left for you to do.

Take over the management of the shipyards yourselves; make the shipyards your own, make the jobs your own, decide the working conditions yourselves, decide your wages yourselves.

In Russia the masters refused to give their slaves a living wage, too. The Russian workers put aside the bosses and their tool, the Russian Government, and took over industry in their own interests.

There is only one way out, a nation-wide general strike with its object the overthrow of the present rotten system which produces thousands of millionaires and millions of paupers each year.

The Russians have shown you the way out. What are you going to do about it? You are doomed to wage slavery till you die unless you wake up, realize that you and the boss have not one thing in common, that the employing class must be overthrown, and that you, the workers, must take over the control of your jobs, and through them the control of your lives, instead of offering yourselves up to the masters as a sacrifice six days a week, so that they may coin profits out of your sweat and toil.

Under the heading: "Strikers to Do Own Policing," the *Union Record* printed a statement issued by the Publicity Division of the Strike Committee. This statement announced that "the personnel of the Executive Strike Committee is at the disposal of organized labour and the *general public*. This committee meets daily at 1:30 in room nine, Labour Temple."

The following significant statement is added:

Relative to reports that Chief of Police Warren planned an increase of the Seattle police force during the strike, the committee announces that there will be absolutely no need of building up a larger *police force organization. The Strike Executive Committee has already perfected plans to do its own policing on behalf of organized labour.* Details of this plan will be announced Tuesday.

Persons having no urgent business to attend to on the streets after 8 o'clock in the evening should *remain at home wherever possible...*The firefighters of Seattle have accordingly been asked to remain at their posts during the strike.

The committee has properly taken care of all laundry work for hospitals by securing one of the largest private laundries in the city, where this work will be done *under the supervision of the committee.* The health and sanitary end has also been adequately *attended to.*

The Executive Committee wishes the public in general to realize that *all matters relating to the general strike are being attended to by the committee in its usual thorough manner. All details large or small receive their attention.*

(*Signed*) Publicity Committee
W. F. DeLancey, Chairman,
W. Z. Zimmer, Secretary.

In Other words, this government within a government, this self-appointed and Hell-anointed Soviet, would take over the policing of the city, would do laundry work, sanitary and health work, and *attend to all details large or small.*

The city government was simply to be supplanted; the soviet told the firemen what to do and notified citizens that Chief Warren need not increase the police force. They would attend to the policing and everything else. They were going to run the government; they were going to supersede the duly-elected officials.

I read their proclamation. Was this Russia or the United States? In scanning the names of the Executive Committee I saw they were, in the main, brainless tools who had been put in the front row to serve the leaders who as yet were under cover and operating by indirection.

Immediately I issued the following statement:

Certain things are necessary to the preservation of life. Water, light, and food are essential. The city government will continue to operate its light and water plants. *It will care for sanitation.* If the men now on the job quit, others will be substituted.

The seat of government is still at the City Hall. The Mayor and the Chief of Police, together with their legally chosen assistants, are the peace officers of this city, and *will continue to police the city of Seattle.* Our function is to preserve order and protect life and property. *This will be done.*   Ole Hanson, *Mayor.*

The time had now come for them to throw off the mask. They had led the deceived rank and file so far that they believed they would now follow the crafty leaders to the end. There was no further concealment in the street propaganda. The talk went up and down the city that this committee of ignoramuses and tools were going to establish a government by themselves and for themselves. As expected, on February fourth, the public announcement of their revolutionary plans appeared in the *Union Record*. This was done in order to prepare the people for the establishment *and continuance of the control of the soviet*. It was considered carefully and Anna Louise Strong was chosen to write the editorial and thus prepare the minds of the people in order to lessen the shock.

The *Record* editorial was captioned:

THURSDAY AT 10 a. m.

There will be many cheering, and there will be some who fear. Both these emotions are useful, but not too much of either. We are undertaking the most tremendous move ever made by *Labour* in this country, a move which will lead
NO ONE KNOWS WHERE

LABOUR WILL FEED THE PEOPLE
Twelve great kitchens have been offered, and from them food will be distributed by the provision trades at low cost to all.

LABOUR WILL CARE FOR THE BABIES AND THE SICK
The milk-wagon drivers and the laundry drivers are arranging plans for supplying milk to the babies, invalids, and hospitals, and taking care of the cleaning of linen for hospitals.

LABOUR WILL PRESERVE ORDER
The Strike Committee is arranging for guards, and it is expected that the stopping of the cars will keep people at home.

* * * * *

A few hot-headed enthusiasts have complained that strikers only should be fed, and the general public left to endure severe discomfort. Aside from the in humanitarian character of such suggestions, let them get this straight:
NOT THE WITHDRAWAL OF LABOUR POWER, BUT THE POWER OF THE WORKERS TO MANAGE WILL WIN THIS STRIKE

What does Mr. Piez of the Shipping Board care about the closing down of Seattle's shipyards, or even of all the industries of the Northwest? Will it not merely strengthen the yards at Hog Island, in which he is more interested?

When the shipyard owners of Seattle were on the point of agreeing with the workers, it was Mr. Piez who wired them that, if they so agreed —

HE WOULD NOT LET THEM HAVE STEEL
Whether this is camouflage we have no means of knowing. But we do know that the great Eastern combinations of capitalists *could afford* to offer privately to Mr. Skinner, Mr. Ames, and Mr. Duthie a few millions apiece in Eastern shipyard stock,

RATHER THAN LET THE WORKERS WIN

The closing down of Seattle's industries, as a *mere shutdown,* will not affect these Eastern gentlemen much. They could let the whole Northwest go to pieces as far as money alone is concerned.

But, the closing down of the capitalistically controlled industries of Seattle, while the *workers organize* to feed the people, to care for the babies and the sick, to preserve order — *this* will move them, for this looks too much like the taking over of *power* by the workers.

* * * * *

Labour will not only *shut down* the industries, but' Labour will *reopen,* under the management of the appropriate trades, such activities as are needed to pre-serve public health and public peace. If the strike continues. Labour may feel led to avoid public suffering by reopening more and more activities,

UNDER ITS OWN MANAGEMENT

And this is why we say we are starting on a road that leads —
NO ONE KNOWS WHERE!

The editorial speaks for itself. No comment is necessary. The guilty coward leaders hiding in the background had prepared a dummy committee, and with the help of their propaganda sheet now proposed to *do as planned in Linnton and take over all industry, all civil authority, and follow exactly the same course as was followed in Russia.*

On the day before the strike Leon Green, Russian alien and bolshevist, gave out the following interview:

The members of the Electrical Workers' Local 77 at a meeting last night *ex-pressed regret that the first vote on the general strike was not unanimous.* They then voted *unanimously to order off every member of the Union employed by the city, Puget Sound Traction, Light and Power Company* and other concerns at 10 o'clock to-morrow morning. This means that every electrician in the city will quit.

It will affect the *fire alarm, city light, telegraph, and telephone companies.* The intention of the Union is to make the tie-up so complete that the strike will not last twenty-four hours...*Pulling off the electrical workers in charge of the fire alarm system will make useless the effort of the city to stay on the job.*

The Union appointed a committee of three, composed of Leon Green, alien; Hulet M. Wells, already under sentence; and "Red" O'Neil, with power to act on all matters affecting the electrical workers during the strike.

I immediately called a meeting, in my office, of all the department heads, notified them neither to ask for nor accept any exemption; to conduct the city's business as formerly, and discipline according to civil service rules all employees who struck.

A secret meeting of I.W.W.s was interrupted by the entrance of A. E. Miller. He immediately spoke and said: "I can stay here but a few moments. Some-one has notified the International of our plans. The International vice-

47

president is on his way here. Some dirty rat has reported that we are I.W.W., and if the vice-president got the evidence, we would certainly have to go. You know what that means; the strike is broken if we are removed. Don't give any evidence connecting us with the I.W.W."

The International vice-president did come and some time thereafter Miller was removed from the Engineers Local by action of the International. At the time this is being written, the case is in court.

On February fifth, the day before the general strike, I was called on the telephone and asked to talk with several conservative labour leaders at the Metal Trades Council. Some of the men named were real loyal citizens, and I at once walked over to their headquarters two blocks away. As soon as I arrived I found a gathering consisting of Hulet M. Wells, Anna Louise Strong, and several others. They asked if we could not come to an arrangement whereby the city employees might walk out and the light plant be shut down. In a few words I told them they were revolutionists, not strikers; had no grievance against the city, and that the city utilities would function as long as we had one man who would work and one rifle to protect him. I then left.

At 10 o'clock that night Frank Rust called me on the 'phone and said that if I would come down to the Labour Temple the whole Strike Committee would meet me, and he felt sure an understanding could be reached. I told him it was useless. He said: "Mayor, come down for the sake of conservative labour." I was very busy working in my bedroom on plans for defence, including securing cartridges, shot guns, machine guns, drawing a map showing the places where the men were to be stationed, and massing our forces at what I considered strategic points. I may say in passing that the Labour Temple would have been our uptown headquarters within thirty minutes after trouble started and that the very nest where this hellish plot was hatched would have been the place where the dead would have been prepared for later burial.

After Rust pleaded with me I called for my car and went to the Labour Temple and was immediately conducted into a secret meeting. While there certain members of the Strike Committee tried to get me to agree to various proposals. One was that they were to allow the men to remain at work in our light plant, but that they had plenty of men who could quietly and secretly cut off lights from all stores, factories, etc., and that I should make public statements but should not interfere. I told them that the light and street cars and municipal affairs would continue to function; that any man who interfered would be shot; that they were revolutionists, and we would not concede anything to them. Speaker after speaker rose to his feet and declared the city utilities were theirs; that they represented the workers, and they *only* were to be considered. I told them: "The city utilities belong to all the people, not to any class. They will function for all the people. Any force necessary will be used to continue their operation."

Leon Green then rose and said: "What is the use of talking to Hanson? Why trim around? He has told you plainly that he will run every public utility. I

48

know him well enough to know that he means it. Now, if we have the greater force, he will go down. If he has the greater force, he will win. The issue is plain." I said: "Green, you understand the situation and so do I. When Americanism is the issue there can be no compromise. Go to it. Do your worst. We defy you and all your kind, and remember this, that even if you clean us up [city authorities], back of us stands the whole Government of this country. But, in my best judgment, we will win without government aid, because the people of this city are back of the city authorities."

I then left them and went to my home to work. I had already wired Secretary of War Baker, stating exact conditions in Seattle, and asked him to stand ready with government troops in case the revolutionists were able to win from the city authorities. We also communicated with Governor Lister, who was then very ill, President Suzzalo and Attorney General Vaugn Tanner having charge of his affairs, and asked that the troops be called, stationed in the armoury and Fort Lawton and held in readiness in case we proved unable to handle the situation.

The troops, old regulars who had seen service, came quickly to Seattle, were stationed in the armoury, and remained there during the entire trouble. The business community, many of them, were very much alarmed and wanted martial law. Some believed that only government troops could handle the situation, but good old Chief Warren was busy. We swore in hundreds of emergency policemen, armed them and stood ready. The Chief secured machine guns, mounted them on trucks, and enlisted the services of discharged soldiers who had handled the same guns on the Flanders front. We had dozens of motor cars ready; the morale of the police was 100 per cent. Lieutenant Hedges had been in the army. He drilled his men night and day. On February sixth he was made captain. Every policeman in Seattle stood ready to die in his tracks before he went back one inch. And the Irish, God bless them, we literally had to confine these boys in the assembly room, so anxious were they to clean out the Reds! For years before I was mayor, the Reds had called the police dirty rats, dogs, capitalist tools; they had pushed them off the sidewalks, and when they had arrested a Red, they had been suspended. It was different now. Both the Chief and I told them we would go all the way with them, that an order issued meant that they were to execute it and that no skim-milk measures would go. They cheered and waited. Seattle has 450 policemen of whom every man is loyal and true, Catholic or Protestant, Jew or Gentile, "and that goes."

In the meantime, the people of Seattle had rushed to the stores and purchased hundreds of dollars' worth of needful articles. Believing that the lights would go out, whole stocks of lamps were disposed of. On February fifth there was no store in the entire city that could wait on one fifth of its customers. It was as if every house was to be quarantined and each household must live within itself for many days. In the gray dawn of the morning of February sixth army truck after army truck filled with regular troops from Camp Lewis rumbled through the city, and *we were ready*.

Chapter Five - Revolution Started and Stopped in Seattle

At TEN o'clock, February sixth, a strange silence fell over our city of four hundred thousand people. Streetcar gongs ceased their clamour; newsboys cast their unsold papers into the street; from the doors of mill and factory, store and workshop, streamed sixty-five thousand workmen. School children with fear in their hearts hurried homeward. *The life stream of a great city stopped.*

The mass strike, most potent weapon of revolutionists, was in operation.

Merchants, bankers, tradesmen, preachers, lawyers, doctors, and workers stood in silence with questioning looks on their faces. It was as if a great earthquake was expected from which none could escape.

Without reason — without cause — our city lay prostrate.

The criminal leaders of union labour issued their ukase, refusing to allow any one to do anything in any way without first securing their august permission, evidenced by a printed slip, marked "exemption." They announced that only a few exemptions would be granted. They would bury the dead if the hearse and automobile owners gave them half the profits; they would allow hospitals to operate if exemption was applied for; but light, transportation, and food for stores or restaurants were not exempted.

They said: "We will run our soup houses and that is all we will do."

They graciously permitted the sale of a ration of milk for all bottle-fed babies. They demanded that our municipal utilities should cease to be. They openly advocated the taking over of all enterprises.

Leon Green said to me on the day of the strike: "You shall have no light and no power. Your streets shall be dark. Hospitals cannot function. We will make it so terrible that in a short time we will win."

I replied: "We shall have light and water and transportation. Our municipal activities shall not cease. This is America and not Russia. You and your anarchists shall not control this Government."

Thus we defied them. Their plans were carefully laid. The Soldiers, Sailors, and Workmen's Council had been organized to have super-control of all things. Different crafts were to conduct each industry. Confiscation and reappropriation were at hand, they thought. They believed that because of the response to the general strike order, the workmen of Seattle were revolutionists and would assist in the overthrow of the Government. Of course, I remained at the City Hall with my secretary, directing our preparations. My problem was to strike at the psychological time. I felt that the people needed a little time really to sense what was going on. We were prepared and could wait. Our main fight was to continue the operation of the light plant in order that the city should not be thrown into darkness.

I called about me the employees of the light department, and standing on a table, told them exactly what the plan was and how they, by leaving their posts, would be assisting the revolutionists and turning the city over to the thugs and blacklegs, who would loot, rape, and kill, and establish a reign of terror. Despite enormous pressure, the great majority remained on the job, while the places of the few who left were immediately filled by volunteers who had worked at similar occupations in days gone by. Practically every business house in Seattle closed, several through fear, although they had sufficient help on hand to remain open. All restaurants were closed, while the soup houses established by the strikers were a complete failure.

As I walked up Second Avenue the afternoon of February sixth a funeral passed by and on the hearse, in large letters, were the words:

Exempted by the Strike Committee

The victims of the "flu" epidemic could not be buried without the permission of this august body! But still I waited. I felt that the public had not suffered sufficiently, as yet, to cause them to turn upon the usurpers.

On the morning of the seventh no newspapers had as yet appeared. The only authentic printed word on the situation to reach the people came from Portland, Oregon, when the *Oregonian* was offered on the streets. So eager were the people for something official that all copies of the *Oregonian* were sold out half an hour after reaching the city. A rumour would start, and in an hour spread all over the city. Some strike sympathizers went from house to house, telling the people the headworks of the water plant had been dynamited. Others announced that the city would be in darkness that night; others that the Mayor had been assassinated.

As the first day of the strike came to a close, the city of Seattle was in a state of unrest, while many of its people feared nightfall, shuddering to think of what might follow the failure of the lights to "come on." Women kept calling up the city authorities, pleading for protection. I received one message notifying me that I would suffer the consequences unless I removed from my motor car the small American flag that flew above the radiator. I answered this coward simply by covering the entire top of my car with a larger flag, and from that time on drove the streets of Seattle with Old Glory above me.

The municipal street cars did not run the first day, although Thos. F. Murphine, Superintendent of Public Utilities, was anxious to operate them. The Chief of Police believed that running the street cars would bring many women and children down town and that if a riot occurred many innocent folks might be shot down. The sidewalks were thronged with strikers, but there was a noticeable absence of women and children. That night the city lights continued burning. I stood and watched the lights hour after hour, wondering whether they would continue sending out their beams to give hope and protection to our citizens. They did continue to burn, and the general strike never succeeded in stopping the flow of one drop of water, nor was it able to keep from burning one single eightcandle-power light, while gas flowed through the mains without any interruption whatever.

At ten o'clock the next morning (the seventh), I decided that the psychological time had come to take the offensive, and sat down to my typewriter and wrote the following proclamation to the people of Seattle:

Proclamation to the People of Seattle:

By virtue of the authority vested in me as mayor, I hereby guarantee to all the people of Seattle absolute and complete protection. They should go about their daily work and business in perfect security. We have fifteen hundred policemen, fifteen hundred regular soldiers from Camp Lewis, and can and will secure, if necessary, every soldier in the Northwest to protect life, business, and property.

The time has come for every person in Seattle to show his Americanism. Go about your daily duties without fear. We will see that you have food, transportation, water, light, gas, and all necessities. The anarchists in this community shall not rule its affairs. All persons violating the laws will be dealt with summarily.

Ole Hanson, Mayor.

I then prepared an ultimatum to the Executive Strike Committee, demanding unconditional, complete, and unequivocal surrender and notifying them that if the strike was not called off the following day, I would take advantage of the offer of the U.S. Government and operate all essential industries. I instructed my secretary to serve this notice on the Strike Committee at once.

I then rushed copies of both to L. Roy Sanders, managing editor of the *Seattle Star,* who was determined to go to press and issue his paper. At my request he gave up practically his entire front page to the proclamation and ultimatum. Loyal union men, obeying the orders of their International, printed the paper, and alongside the proclamation was printed a picture of the Stars and Stripes. The date line read: "Seattle, United States of America."

Exactly at noon Mr. Conklin, my secretary, entered the room of the Executive Strike Committee at the Labour Temple and asked if this was the General Executive Strike Committee. The chairman responded that it was and asked: "What do you want?" He then told them that he had a message from the Mayor, and continued: "In order to be sure you all understand it, I will read it." As he read the ultimatum, pausing between the sentences, he noticed the faces of the very men who had been loudest in "egging on" the workers turn pale. They knew we were prepared and that we proposed to go the full limit in defeating their nefarious and un-American aims.

While the *Seattle Star* was striving, under police protection, to get out their newspaper, a committee consisting of eight or nine labour leaders, including "Jimmy" Duncan, Hulet M. Wells, and E. A. Miller, came to the mayor's office and asked for a consultation. This was about eleven thirty. I told them to wait in my office until I returned, as I had important business to attend to. I let them wait there until three o'clock that afternoon, without lunch and without any communication with their friends on the outside. Before they could get away to rally their followers the *Seattle Star,* containing my proclamation, had distributed free, under police protection, 100,000 copies of the paper, and *I knew then that the attempted revolution was crushed.*

At three o'clock I came back to my office and in the presence of two citizens whom I had called in the committee were told that we had nothing to say to them, that we would not deal with revolutionists. Duncan pleaded for help to get the leaders "out of the hole." He wanted some promise, some little thing to show to the strikers, in order that he. Wells, Miller, *et al.* might not lose their prestige. We absolutely refused to consider anything but complete and unconditional surrender. Duncan said: "Don't be too sure about the troops. It is about an even break whether they go with you or with us. We don't want to make the test"; and I told him that nothing would please me better than to have the test come, "the quicker, the better"; that if our soldiers were not loyal, the country could not stand, but "you will find that the soldiers will fight for the flag in Seattle just as quickly as they did across the seas." The meeting then broke up and from that day to the time I left the mayor's office he never set foot inside the door again.

With my proclamation occupying most of the front page of the *Star,* our police from their motor trucks had spread the paper broadcast over the city, and within fifteen minutes after the first paper was given away, 250 Elks came in a body to my office, offering their support and assistance. Literally thousands of Seattle citizens of all walks of life hurried to the City Hall and offered their services. Thomas F. Murphine, my friend and appointee as Superintendent of Public Utilities, ran the first municipal street car through the public streets, unguarded and unafraid.

I gave orders to shoot on sight any lawbreaker attempting to create a riot, and Joel Warren, chief of police, a dead shot and a true man, stood ready with fifteen hundred men under him to quell disorder. We used no soldiers for any purpose, either as guards or policemen, although fifteen hundred stood ready to help. No martial law was declared. The American spirit of our people burst into flame and the bolsheviki, the I.W.W.'s, the internationalists, the traitors — all of them cowards — crowded the railway stations and wharves to make their escape. Seattle stood four square and loyal, and in my judgment, its citizenship and its love of country prevented the spread of the Hell-inspired doctrines of Lenin and Trotsky.

The Traction Company officials came to my bedside (I was quite ill) and asked if I wished them to run their cars. I not only told them I wished their cars to be run, but demanded that they commence operation at once. They were willing, and Superintendent G. A. Richardson of the Puget Sound Traction, Light, and Power Co., took out the company's first car, and clanging the bell, ran up and down Second Avenue.

The operation of the street cars was the finish of the strike, and despite the frenzied orders of the Bolshevist chiefs, the workers everywhere returned to their work. *The strike was over.* The attempted revolution was a failure and yet, the men who led this Bolshevist uprising are free men to-day. It is true a few lodging-house I.W.W.'s were arrested and charged with "criminal anarchy" under the state law, but the leaders have never been arrested and have never been prosecuted by any one.

At this writing James Duncan is still secretary of the Central Labour Council, advocating the "one big union" to provide the mass organization to overthrow our Government, and on September fourteenth President Wilson received him as a representative of Labour at the Washington Hotel in Seattle.

Hulet M. Wells and Sam Sadler are in prison, serving sentences imposed upon them long before the Seattle strike occurred. Strong efforts are being made — as I write — to persuade President Wilson to open the doors of the penitentiary for them. If Wells and Sadler and men of their stripe are released, the efforts of law-enforcing officials will be laughed at in this country. If they should be freed, then every criminal in every jail and penitentiary in the land should also walk out free. There are excuses and reasons for men committing breaches of the law against one another, but there can be no excuse, no palliation, for the men who, during our time of trouble, when our boys were fighting in the trenches across the seas, strove to hamper and destroy the Government of our country — activities which if successful meant not only chaos at home, but defeat, imprisonment, suffering, and death for the boys across the water.

Leon Green, Russian alien bolshevist (right name Leon Butowsky) has never been even arrested, although he openly advocated forcible overthrow of our Government. The city government can prosecute men only on minor charges, such as disorderly conduct, etc., but it does seem as if the National Government could find, arrest, and punish men like him.

While the others trimmed and misrepresented their objects in the general strike, Leon Green told the truth, and gloried in the telling. He was for force and said it should be used. He cared not for suffering, and said so. He was perfectly willing that the folks in hospitals should die from want of heat, food, medical attendance, nursing, etc. He wanted the city in darkness, and said so. Other cowards who worked with him talked all these things in private, but camouflaged in public. Leon was born in Russia, hated our Government, and expected and helped plan its overthrow. He left Seattle and escaped. Nothing more has been heard of him. The authorities cannot find him. Well, I will tell them where he is and what he is doing. He is business agent of two different retail clerks' unions in Chicago. He hands out his cards every day of the month. He walks the streets unmolested and unafraid. He is still working to overthrow our Government.

Here is a copy of his card, with his address and telephone number:

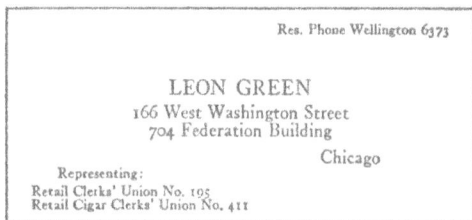

```
                                        Res. Phone Wellington 6373

                        LEON GREEN
                    166 West Washington Street
                    704 Federation Building
                                              Chicago
          Representing:
    Retail Clerks' Union No. 105
    Retail Cigar Clerks' Union No. 411
```

Of course I am telling this in confidence. I trust no one will inform the hard-searching sleuths where he can be found.

E. B. Ault is still editor of the *Union Record* and still attacks the United States Government, decent men (and their families) nightly. The Central Labour Council of Seattle still functions as a bolshevist organization. When the vote was taken as to whether or not to strike on the Fourth of July (the Mooney tie-up) the vote stood 76 for and 67 against. The reason it was lost was not because of a desire to abandon the I.W.W. propaganda, but because the shipyard owners of Seattle let it be known that if the strike vote was successful their yards would close and not reopen for several months.

Every Wednesday night anarchy, sabotage, and disloyalty are openly preached in the Labour Temple in Seattle, while the preaching and teaching of anarchy, syndicalism, sabotage, and bolshevism is being carried on throughout the nation, and hundreds of tons of bolshevist propaganda continue to be distributed. I go to our book-stores and the shelves groan with hundreds of pamphlets denouncing our Government and praising the Soviet Government of Russia. I pick up a *Social Service Bulletin* published in New York City (Grace Scribner, editor) and find the leading contributor on the Seattle strike to be an I.W.W. organizer of Local 500. On the back page I find a list of numerous bolshevik publications, with the addresses where they can be secured. Touring the country from one end to the other are prominent camouflaged traitors who describe in glowing terms the wonderful government of soviet Russia, while the loyal people of the United States sit idly by and allow the opponents of our Government to use the printed word to destroy our Government and do not furnish truthful literature to combat it.

The working men of Seattle were imposed upon by their bolshevist leaders. There were on strike about 65,000 union men and approximately 75,000 men and women who were unorganized. The loss to the workers in wages alone amounted to $3,735,000, but the loss to the cause of Labour cannot be measured in dollars and cents.

Capital has been charged, and is oft-times guilty, of exploiting Labour, but in Seattle the I.W.W. leaders of Labour have exploited it for revolutionary ends and held back the progress of those who toil. Thus has it ever been. Whenever Labour listens to the teachers of anarchy, whenever it obeys the commands of the revolutionaries, it receives a serious setback. Not one International president in the United States approved the general strike. Every agreement made by Labour was treated as a scrap of paper, torn up and thrown aside, and if it had not been for the calling of a great meeting of employers at the Chamber of Commerce, immediately after the strike, at which I and others pleaded with the employers to make no reprisals, every labour organization in the city of Seattle would have been destroyed.

So disastrous was the effect upon the minds of the people of this community that when three decent, fairly conservative labour men became candidates for the City Council on March 15, 1919, and were opposed by three men who had supported the cause of law and order — they were overwhelmingly defeated, polling only a scant 20,000 votes in a city of 400,000, where both men and women vote, and where organized Labour has a membership of more than 60,000.

The attempted revolution is over; the general strike and its results are history, but the battle between the *decent forces of Labour* and the *one big union — I.W.W. element* — has only just begun. That fight must be settled. Either the conservative, constructive forces of Labour must so conduct its affairs that all fair-minded men will respect it; or the forces of revolution will take charge and lead it — *God knows where.*

Chapter Six - Something of the Rise, Trial, and Failure of Bolshevism in Europe

IN ORDER to understand that which is, it is necessary to know what has been. The story of a human being does not begin at the age of twenty-one, but when the first pulse of life feebly throbs in the infant body, months before birth, and never ends until the last feeble gasp. To understand the man of twenty-five it is sometimes very helpful to know the environment of his childhood; to know something of his early struggles and disappointments and his early teachings.

In order really to interpret and sense bolshevism, one must start at its beginning and trace its evolution and development through the years of its existence. Great movements do not come into being without a cause, without leaders, without conscious effort. They don't just happen. Never since the mule driver Mohammed inaugurated his religion has any belief been so thoroughly embedded in the minds of hundreds of thousands as bolshevism is to-day. It has taken possession of Russia, overthrown the wishes of the vast majority of its people, laid desolate its countryside, depopulated its cities, murdered its opponents, starved unnumbered innocents, and yet to-day, as I write, it is in undisputed possession of a large portion of the earth's surface. It has invaded Germany, established itself in Hungary, caused riots in Italy, France, and several other countries in Europe; has crossed the sea and invaded our northern neighbour, Canada, and made a sinister attempt at revolution in our own land. It is apparently as fluid as quicksilver, as cosmopolitan as a Jew, is indigenous to no country or clime, and its rise has been as rapid as its effect has been destructive.

How did it start? Who conceived the idea? What was its cause? What has been its history?

In Torschok, Russia, in the year 1814, Michael Bakounin was born. Of noble parentage, he was educated for the military service and became an officer of artillery before his majority. While stationed in Poland, he became disgusted with Russian militarism, the Russian Government, and its oppression of the poor. He threw up his commission and studied philosophy at St. Petersburg and Berlin. He became a great student of Hegel and Schopenhauer. Hegel was a strong believer in Napoleon, calling him "the universal genius"; Schopenhauer was the prize misanthrope of the ages who held pleasure as merely the absence of pain, believed in nothing or no one, looked on the dark side of every shield, and preached universal unhappiness as a duty. Fit teachers for the father of anarchistic communism, which, as we shall see, developed later into revolutionary syndicalism. A disappointed princeling, not a proletarian, mind you, thought of it first.

In Berlin his time was spent in the revolutionary circles and he came under their influence. From Arnold Ruge, who led an insurrection in Dresden in 1848, he imbibed the doctrines of communism, advocating the return to that primal society which was first established on earth and known as the Commune.

The Commune is society's primary organic cell. It is a political body which regulates all the local interests of its inhabitants. The Commune is derived from the French word *"Comun,"* meaning: "the common people," says the Dictionary of Vital Economy, edited by Inglis Palgrave. (Vol. I, p. 360.)

It would indeed be difficult to define the more modern soviet in other terms than those used in defining the Commune. They are one and the same.

Prince Bakounin, after becoming thoroughly impregnated with the principles of the return to the first primitive society, advanced one stage further which led him to embrace anarchy itself.

Proudhun at that time was the dominating intellectual figure of anarchy and revolution in France, and from Proudhun the princeling absorbed the principles of anarchy; but so strongly had communism been impressed upon him that he forebore to throw it entirely overboard. He united the two into a kind of a no-law-much-law combination, the hybrid product resulting in what is known as anarchistic communism.

Ruge, from whom Bakounin imbibed his communism, wanted to return to the first organized society. Proudhun, on the other hand, went one step further back in the realm of history, and his idea, stripped to the skeleton, was the return to the first condition of man which was, of course, the unrestrained, unruled, undeveloped anarchy of the first man, before society had any organization whatever. He said: "Government of man in every form is oppression. The highest perfection of society is found in the union of order and anarchy." Of course this is a paradoxical, impossible situation. If you have organized society, you have no anarchy. In fact, if you have order, a government must be in control to maintain it; but a little truth such as this never bothered Proudhun or Bakounin or any of their followers from that day to this.

Bakounin, after a career which inflamed large portions of Europe, took part in the great Dresden Insurrection of 1848. He was arrested and condemned to death, but was later returned to the Russian authorities and banished to

Siberia. He escaped from Siberia through Japan, came to the United States, and in 1861 returned to London to preach his theory of revolution. As he grew older he became more demented, if such a thing could be, and supported every propaganda of revolution in every country he visited.

He fought Marx and his theories to a standstill, causing Marx to call the International Congress at The Hague in order to prevent Bakounin from attending, as he was subject to arrest and imprisonment in all countries of Europe except Switzerland. The doctrines of Marx were triumphant at this congress. Communistic anarchy met its defeat, although the doctrines of Marx and Bakounin were more or less of the same bolt of cloth, both believing in communism. As a matter of fact, communism was the early name for socialism. The ends sought were practically identical, but there was a difference in the methods.

The General Council was then transferred to our own land (New York City), and in a short time met a painless and unregretted death. Bakounin, however, refused to accept his defeat at the hands of the Marxists and called another international congress in Switzerland which also met with failure.

The communistic anarchists believed in the destruction of the state absolutely and completely — they wanted no government except the government of the shop. Marx wanted, by political action, to take possession of the machinery of the state and use the state to inaugurate a socialistic regime. Just what that regime was to be has ever been a nebulous, very much unknown and very much disagreed upon matter. Each socialist from that day to this has builded his own ideas of the manner in which socialism was to be conducted, very much as the peoples of the world have built their own Heaven in the future world: the Esquimaux believing it to be a place of warmth with plenty of whale oil to drink; the Indian picturing it as the happy hunting grounds; the Mohammedan as a place of wonderful houris and thousands of slaves. Most people, however, agree upon it being a place where there is but little to do and eternity to do it in.

It may well be said that while there was a difference in the rules of the game then as now, it was the same old game of taking away what belonged to someone else, without compensation, for the benefit of either individuals or groups of individuals who possessed nothing and wanted something. This fundamental exists in the teachings of all the isms and runs like a red thread through the statements of the aims of most of them. Apparently they make the great mistake, unconsciously, of believing that the wealth of the world is a certain, definite, existing entity requiring only a new distribution to cure the ills of man. Of course, the wealth of the world is an ever-changing, constantly renewing thing; brought into being by the application of human labour and thought to the raw resources of the earth. In no other way was wealth ever produced and in no other way can it ever be created. However, we digress; let us get back to Bakounin and Proudhun and France, where the new thought was receiving its first trial in the actual affairs of life.

It may well be said that the methods used to bring about anarchistic communism, or syndicalism, were not the brain-child of any one man, nor were they worked out in the libraries of economic schools. The application of the nearest at hand and most agitated procedure for the meeting of economic conditions at a particular time and particular place was always used. Syndicalism has the background of experience and its success or failure has long ceased to be a matter of experiment. It has been tried repeatedly and has failed ingloriously, even after securing the complete overthrow of existing governments; and, as we will see later, its successful coup in Russia gives additional proof to the world that it will not work and cannot work. Human nature in its most vital depths cannot be changed by a proclamation or a speech. Syndicalism is to-day the most stupendous failure in government of all history.

Proudhun was a college-bred young man and became one of the great characters of his time. His philosophy was taken from Hegel and Adam Smith. He believed in a redistribution of wealth and one of the first measures he introduced in the Assembly of the Seine, to which he was elected in 1848, was a measure whereby one third of the rent, interest, and profit was to be taken away from its possessors. This was rejected by the Assembly. One good thing, however, may be said of this anarchist and that is, he was free from any feelings of personal hate and did not teach the doctrine of personal hatred against the fortunate possessors of wealth.

Proudhun became the leader of those who would innovate and change the existing order of things. The question before France was its rehabilitation. Socialism had been advocated in France theretofore, but received its greatest impetus at that time. "Civil liberty for all" became the battle-cry. The absence of civil liberty was pointed out by all radicals and a return to the conditions of prehistoric man and his full liberties was advocated. Rousseau, long before, had urged full political liberty for all mankind on the theory that each man being a part of the community should have his say as to the conduct of that community.

In passing, it may be recalled that in our own country at that time (1848) slavery reigned triumphant over the most fertile, settled part of the Union and there were comparatively few men who advocated complete and immediate abolition of that evil.

In France this doctrine of equality gained adherents rapidly because *misgovernment caused discontent and because all men in all times have dreamed and desired equality and freedom.* Of course, the dreams of reform left unsatisfied led to the advocacy of insurrection. The hurry-up, get-it-over-quick zealots brought on chaos instead of a constructive policy. The revolt was openly preached; the repressive and neglectful government added oil to the fires, and the reign of Louis Philippe brought weakness and do-nothingness. Contempt instead of allegiance was stimulated. The rotting out of the old institutions of State and Church brought widespread distrust and rebellion. Some other form of government was needed. The result was that the one most exploited was adopted. Frenchmen of that age said: "Nothing can be worse than what we have. Let us try." Other nations cleaned out and cleaned up, but the rulers of France slept on, lacking the vision and courage to change the existing order to meet the views of the moderately liberal who are always in the majority in every land.

At this time industry in France and the other Latin countries of Europe was in the primary state of organization — in England and the United States it was very much farther advanced. It may be said that industrialism in France in 1840 occupied about the same plane of development as that of Russia in 1917. It was inchoate, unformed, undeveloped. The main industries were conducted in small shops; five or ten or twenty workmen under one master. This disconnection undoubtedly gave form to the "one shop, one vote" rule, which then, as now, was the teaching of the syndicalist. The absolute futility of political effort was preached on every corner and in every pamphlet. The overthrow of the government was openly advocated. Strike after strike was inaugurated, finally culminating in 1848 in a general strike and the overturning of the government. Under the new socialistic regime happiness, contentment, and prosperity had been promised and the people, believing the promises, had acted accordingly.

Just as soon as the new government took charge the people demanded of the government the right to work. The government immediately instituted great systems of public workshops to provide employment and produce something. Thrifty men and women with songs on their lips and joy in their hearts went to work, believing that the millennium had come. The lazy, the loafer, the agitator, did not go to work but immediately began another agitation that unemployment insurance should be furnished them. Thirty sous per day was to be the pension for doing nothing — forty sous the reward for work.

The unemployed increased miraculously overnight. The thrifty and industrious then saw that they were supporting the no-goods and do-nothings and they finally declared that as those who do not work receive thirty sous a day and we who work receive but forty sous a day, we will do only ten sous' worth of work a day, the difference between idleness and effort!

People became discontented and hungry because production was restricted and men looked upon the government as a sort of perpetual and self-perpetuating Christmas tree, which had only to be shaken to bring presents sufficient for the maintenance of all. They forgot, as apparently do many of our later-day social evangelists, that the government is a pauper and only maintains itself on what you and I furnish it. When our contributions cease, government must cease. The places where the coin was distributed became the centres of enormous mobs of unemployed. People fought for places in the ever-lengthening lines of pensioners.

Then the development of land projects was decided upon, but still production decreased and the unemployed increased! Want, hunger, and suffering became universal until finally the very crowds which had demanded revolution forced their way into the Assembly Chamber, declared the socialistic scheme a complete and ignominious failure, and demanded its cessation! The leaders who brought about the experiment were the loudest in denouncing its failure.

The new government did as requested, acceded to the people's demands, reduced and finally suppressed the public works, declaring that they demoralized the people and were a complete failure. The decision brought on a bloody insurrection which was suppressed only after several days of street fighting. The leaders of the revolt, in order to save themselves from their infuriated followers, escaped to foreign lands, there to prepare their alibis and excuses. The cause of honest labour received a setback from which it did not recover for a quarter of a century.

Louis Napoleon was then inaugurated President of the Republic, and in order to save France from starvation, used the credit of the country and embarked upon gigantic schemes of public works which rebuilt a large portion of Paris and provided employment for many who otherwise would have died from starvation. Thus ended, in complete and disastrous failure, the first great experiment in *creating wealth by law instead of by work.*

The stark truth stands out in all history that every class which has emancipated itself *did so by evolution and not by revolution.* The memory of failure, however, usually lasts but a few short years; another generation and the same old Utopian dreams of bygone days are rejuvenated under different leaders and different names and the futile struggle is continued.

People do learn from experience, but only from their own experience. Seldom are the experiences of others in other days accepted as a guide. There are so many explainers who point out in detail the causes of failure, leaving out the fundamental truth, that the thing itself was wrong to start with.

"Syndicalism aims at the federation of workers in all trades into an effective body for the purpose of enforcing the demands of Labour by means of sympathetic strikes," says the New Standard Dictionary. The substitution of "direct action" in place of "sympathetic strikes" makes the definition more comprehensive.

A. D. Lewis defines syndicalism, in "Syndicalism and the General Strike," as "aiming at replacing an economic hierarchy by a system in which different kinds of work are regarded as being of one value, and where there is brotherhood instead of mastery and subservience. It recommends immediate aggression without *carefully planning what is to be done after the victory is won."*

Syndicalism is the doctrine of direct action, principally through *sabotage and the general strike,* inaugurated for the purpose of abolishing private rights, private property, and all government and taking over control of all things by the minority. It stands for a vote for each industry instead of a vote for each human being. It makes the shop or syndicate the local unit of government and a combination of the shops the general governing body.

Syndicat in French simply means "a labour union." In its final analysis, syndicalism is a *government of the trades unions,* no one else having any voice in

61

the government. It is essentially a rule of the minority, as well as a revolutionary organization advocating class war. It teaches sabotage and destruction of our present system by force, recognizing no act as wrong so long as it injures some one or some thing and hampers existing institutions. It repudiates the State, God, and good; despises and abstains from political action; desires by force to overthrow existing governments, but has no agreed-upon plan for conducting government after its overthrow. It is more or less a return to the no-government plan of the first man on earth; lack of compulsion or lack of government being widely preached. It always becomes popular when an agitating minority, desiring to possess the fruits of the efforts of the majority, find it impossible to secure control politically. Still desirous of possession, they try to gain it by direct action, force, sabotage, and the general strike is used to overthrow the government which protects private rights and enforces order.

All men intrusted with the maintenance of order, the police, the army, the navy, the executive officials of city, state, and nation, are considered by syndicalists as the arch enemies of progress. They are hated, lied about, and, if possible, destroyed. All syndicalists are against preparedness and armed forces, because their doctrine of forcible overthrow always fails when met with a greater force. They would disarm the world and abolish authority and all means of self-defence in order to bring about a successful revolution. They would weaken the majority to such an extent that their minority can prevail. All moral law is called bourgeois morality and is to be ridiculed and disobeyed. Instead the moral fibre of mankind must be destroyed. Religion and its teachings must fall and a code of scoundrelism take its place. Open denunciation of the marriage relation is one of the essentials, while free love is almost universally advocated, and, where opportunity offers, practised.

As we know, the only way a minority can rule is by the disfranchisement and repression of the majority; by the establishment of an autocratic rule supported by an army; by the repression or destruction of the unarmed and unready population. Such a rule was the government of the Romanoffs of Russia. It lasted a long time. Such a government has since been established out of the embers of the Russian Revolution by Lenin and Trotsky. Its length of rule depends upon the size and morale of its army, temporarily; on starvation and want, primarily.

As we have seen, the methods of production instituted by the workers in France in the form of government workshops, etc., met with complete failure. Ism authors place the responsibility for failure — "1st, upon the ignorance of the masses; 2nd, upon the selfishness of individuals; 3rd, upon the lack of capital and credit." I quote this from Levine, the socialist author who wrote "French Syndicalism." Strange that capital and credit, the bane of the revolutionary ism-ist, should have been found at all essential! Strange that human selfishness and mass ignorance could not be abolished by ukase!

Upon the complete breakdown of syndicalism in 1848, the workmen of France and England and Germany turned to internationalism as an escape from failure nationally. "We failed," they argued, "because other countries were not doing what we were doing, but were proceeding under the old system. We could not exist alone. We must establish internationalism in all government and industry." Can it be that the Russian bolshevist agitates in every country for the same reason?

The revolutionist argues: "We must place the workers of every country on an equality; one must receive as much as the other in order that there be no advantage between brothers." Of course, they never advertise the fact that costs of living in different countries might make the wage smaller or larger, although the money unit be the same, nor apparently do they take into consideration the fact that a country rich in natural resources and favoured by climate and transportation facilities might produce a great deal more with a great deal less labour. These things they may know, but they never talk about them in public; it would hurt their argument.

The International was formed in 1864, Karl Marx becoming its first great leader. It was composed of French syndicalists, German socialists, and English trade unionists. It had no common programme, but its members were united in discontent over existing conditions. Karl Marx, socialist, and Prince Bakounin communistic-anarchist, or syndicalist, led two opposing factions; Marx advocating the capture of government by orderly political methods, the prince demanding its violent overthrow. United as to the necessity and righteousness of stealing, but divided as to the methods of theft!

The first International advocated direct action, saying it might assume various forms, such as strike, boycott, union label, and sabotage. They preached the strike, not only as a means to better conditions, but for the purpose of harming the employing class and creating and fomenting discontent and class hatred among the workers. The boycott also was advocated as an effective method of forcing employers to terms. Sabotage consists in obstructing in all possible ways the regular process of production to the disadvantage of the employer. It includes destruction of property, intimidation of employers, employees, and the public, wasting materials, etc. It really has the same meaning as the well-known Scotch word "Ca'cannie."

To strike and then strike again seemed to be the main plan then as now. The great strike was to be the last strike and was to bring about revolution and overthrow government. What else the success of the general strike would bring about was left to each one's individual fancy and the whims of inexperienced and unable dictators.

The development of revolutionary syndicalism apparently was the kind of movement suited to the French temperament, which, as Weill points out in his "History of the Social Movement of France," "is far more capable of a single great effort than of continuous and plodding toil." The Latin races usually reject with scorn small but constant progress, preferring the catastrophic, far-off, soap-bubble-hued achievements.

The fact that industrialism had been far more backward in the Latin countries than in England and the United States also encouraged the idea of government by shops; there being thousands of little establishments with a master in charge while in more advanced industrial countries thousands worked in one factory.

Levine in his book on "Syndicalism in France" states:

The French syndicalists recognize that they lack method, persistence, and foresight, although they are sensitive, impulsive, and combative. Many *syndicats* are loosely held together and are easily dissolved. They are composed of a more or less variable and shifting membership. A disorganized *syndicat* generally leaves behind a handful of militant working men, determined to keep up the syndicalist movement. This necessarily brings the *syndicats* into conflict with the State. The result is a feeling of bitterness among the working men toward the army, the police, and the Government in general. The ground is thus prepared for anti-militaristic, anti-state, and anti-patriotic ideas.

In England the situation was different. Prior to the industrial revolution in England, the craft unions were very strong and numerous. Continuous development took place but it was very slow, the workers forming trade unions which were simply combinations of the working men of *one particular trade*. This particular method of collective bargaining held its own for many years and the development was along those lines instead of along the lines of syndicalism. All members of the unions were skilled workers and it was not until machinery made possible the employment of unskilled, untrained men that the lower strata of labour joined labour organizations. This became essential as any man could supplant a trained worker with a few days' experience. The trades unions developed into a trades union which became a national organization. The builders and weavers pioneered this amalgamation.

Chapter Seven - Some of History's Verdicts on Reformers, Utopias, Trade Unions, and Bolshevism

IN a small town in Wales in 1771 Robert Owen was born. He was put to work when but ten years old and before he was twenty was the manager of a large cotton mill. The memory of his early struggles, however, remained with him. A self-made man, he never forgot his origin. He never said, as so many self-made men do: "I succeeded, I broke through the crust. Why cannot all men do likewise?" Robert Owen realized that the great success he had made was the exception and not the rule and his life was spent in an effort, usually fruitless, to better the conditions of the class of men and women from which he sprang.

Surrounding his establishment (where one of the first spinning machines invented by Arkright was installed), he built pleasure resorts for the purpose of discouraging drunkenness and furnishing the workmen places to play and to learn. At that day and age he made the fight, not against "child labour," but against *infant labour.* Men, women, and children were worse off in many instances than chattel slaves and lived amidst surroundings of filth, ignorance, drunkenness, and immorality He instituted lectures in order to teach the people, few of whom could read, the laws of health and decent conduct. He did more. He stopped the employment of very young children. The homes of the people were wonderfully improved; provisions were supplied at cost to the workers; schools were started and he also *inaugurated old-age pensions and sick benefits.*

In 1826 Sir Robert Owen brought communism to the United States and established a colony at New Harmony, Indiana. This colony was situated on 30,000 acres of land which had previously been somewhat developed by a German colony who sold their entire holdings to Owen. Three thousand acres were already under cultivation, besides a vineyard, several orchards, and many other improvements. There was a total of 27,000 acres of good, rich, undeveloped land to fall back on. The village streets were already laid out and there was a great public square surrounded by large brick buildings, owned by the community. The aim of Owen and his followers was to establish a community where property was *held in common.* All were to share in the common labour and all were to receive a liberal education and have every opportunity for the fullest pursuit of knowledge. The qualifications essential for membership were honesty of purpose, temperance, industry, and cleanliness.

Surely this colony, situated on some of the richest land in the world, had every chance to work out communism if it could be worked out. What happened? Just what always has happened. Some worked and delved while others loafed and did nothing but strive to place the burden of their support upon Owen and the workers!

Owen thought that the colonists were not quite ready for a full experiment, so asked that a constitution be adopted and for three years a near form of communism was to be tried. This was agreed upon. The management was to be a council (soviet) under the absolute control of the colonists.

Experience soon proved that things could not be run in that manner and the members *unanimously requested that Owen be made sole manager.* Then were inaugurated the only prosperous times the colony ever enjoyed. He made the idlers go to work and, for a time, all was a new harmony.

Within a few months, however, disturbances arose; there was a continual dispute about work and about land, with the result that on March 30, 1826, the land was divided into four parts and four associations tried to do the work that one had failed to do. They tried to trade between themselves with a paper currency, but in one year Sir Robert saw his idealistic community resolve itself into a wrangling, quarrelling, disorganized mob. Human nature, ever present, demanded individual reward for effort; the lazy wanted rest and their needs supplied without toil. The same work day did not suit either the industrious or the shiftless. It was found impossible to make men into a common mold either by law or agreement. There was individualism, the fruit of the ages, in every man and woman — hence the failure! Despite this failure at New Harmony, dozens of other experiments were tried in the effort to equalize men by law. Henry Ford says: "History is bunk." The communists evidently think so, too.

Verily there is nothing new under the sun. Styles come in and styles go out. Fifteen years ago Theodore Roosevelt visited Seattle and I bought my first silk hat. When I was elected mayor, I bought another in order to be truly *de rigeur.* I happened to find the old hat, and, much to my surprise, was unable to tell one from the other. The style had gone out and then come back again. This apparently is as true in social reform as it was with my hat.

In 1832 Sir Robert Peel made a strenuous fight against one of the grossest evils of the day. The apprentices in the cotton mills, according to early English descriptions, were kept in a miserable condition. By his effort the first statute in English law in favour of the workers was enacted. All laws theretofore had lengthened hours, made conditions worse instead of better, and invariably had been enacted to favour the employers. Pauper children had been disposed of by the parishes (poor houses) to the employers under the name of "apprentices"; but while they were supposed to be learning a trade, they were really slaves. These poor little children of a century ago were compelled not only to work, but to overwork, as the overseer's pay was based on *what the children did.* They were flogged, placed in irons, and even tortured in order to coin the blood and bones of their frail, emaciated bodies into dirty profits. The Peel Law prohibited the binding out as apprentices of *children under* **nine** *years of age and restricted the hours of labour to twelve hours per day;* forbade night toil, and prescribed religious teaching and an elementary education. A wonderful age to live in where such a law could excite such condemnation and such unstinted praise!

Sir Robert Owen and Sir Robert Peel united their forces and met the arguments of the child murderers who solemnly said it was wrong to forbid the little toilers to work longer than twelve hours as they *would starve unless allowed their freedom to toil.* They also said: "The children will learn bad habits and get into bad company and grow up shiftless if such laws are passed." One cannot but note the similarity of their arguments to those used to-day to "protect" child labour in our own country. One writer said: "This law encourages vice and idleness." It took a quarter of a century of hard work to shorten the hours of labour to sixty-nine per week, and this law applied to cotton mills only.

In 1833 the well-known Factory Act was passed. While the press and pulpits resounded with denunciation of slavery in the West Indies and demanded its destruction, the same powers protected the *factory owner* although the poet Southey declared that "the slave trade is divine mercy compared to our factory system."

However, Lord Ashley, afterward the Earl of Shaftesbury, took the leadership in this humanitarian movement and although despised by his class, fought it to a successful finish, so that no child under nine years of age could be employed *except in a silk mill,* where two hours' schooling a day was made compulsory and night work for any one under eighteen was prohibited. After many years of agitation, the employment of women and of boys under the age of ten, in underground mines, was prohibited!

Apparently every improvement in the working conditions of mankind has been criminally slow and always a matter of compromise and only successful when demanded by practically the whole population. Some day, somewhere, perhaps, employers such as those who fought these reforms will realize the reason why so many working people have transferred the hatred they first felt toward the machines to the employers.

England was the first country where industrialism took a real foothold. England had a great deal of idle capital, thousands of idle men and women, and above all, she led the world in inventive genius.

Arkright invented the water frame which made it possible to spin other threads than linen, his invention Imparting a strength and solidity to the thread.

Hargreaves invented the spinning jenny and Key the flying shuttle. In 1792 our own Eli Whitney invented the cotton gin which revolutionized the cotton-growing industry and made possible an unlimited supply of cotton. Without his invention slavery would have been abolished as an economic waste. Cartwright developed the process whereby falling water would run the looms, and Watt perfected his steam engine to a point where it could be used for power in the mills. It drove spindles, ran spinning machines, etc.

Theretofore the workers had worked in their own homes and Spun and woven by hand. The invention of machinery necessitated a general factory and because of the above-mentioned inventions and many others, the factory system was established. Of course, there had been some factories before, but it was not until this period of development that the *factory system* came into existence.

The factory system changed industry from hand work to machine work and for many weary years the battle was carried on between the workers and the machines. Mills were burned down and riots, disturbances, and bloody street battles took place everywhere. The factory system, however, never wholly replaced the hand workers. In Birmingham, for instance, small cutlery is still made in the homes.

It may well be said that the first organization of labour was by the "boss" himself, in giving each worker certain definite duties to perform which dovetailed one into another. This method taught the workers the power of organization, their dependence on one another, and as they met and worked and talked and argued, they finally evolved the idea that they must have a real organization in order to secure their rights, and in order to keep their wages from falling as the inauguration of the machine made every idle man with but a little training capable of taking their positions. After the trade unions were supplanted by the Trades Union, aggressive and active leaders taught syndicalism, brought about a consolidation of the workers, and frightened the middle class until finally the Government indicted the trades unionists for illegal combinations when they notified their employers of a strike. Strike after strike occurred and they were uniformly unsuccessful, so that by 1834 the Trades Union was gradually losing membership and prestige. The workers then reestablished the trade or craft unions.

In "History of Trade Unionism," by Sidney and; Beatrice Webb, the following comment on the rise and? fall of syndicalism in England is found:

The records of the rise and fall of the "new unionism" of 1830-1834 leave us conscious of a vast enlargement in the ideas of the workers, without any corresponding alteration in their tactics in the field. In council they are idealists, dreaming of a new heaven and a new earth, humanitarians, educationalists, socialists, moralists; in battle they are still struggling, half-emancipated serfs of 1825, armed only with the rude weapons of the strike and the boycott; sometimes feared and hated by the propertied class; sometimes merely despised; always oppressed and miserably poor.

Germany was the most backward of the three great European countries so far as industrialism was concerned. England was becoming industrialized rapidly; her factories ran day and night; the establishment of the Bank of England gave her credit, while her ships carried her goods to every part of the world. She controlled the world markets.

France, to a smaller degree, was becoming industrialized, but Germany, backward, agrarian country with an innate attachment to the soil, with a people opposed to change and having very few markets for her goods, lagged far behind. For a score of years Germany was even behind France in the adoption of machinery and the factory system.

Marxism had now become the Bible of many Germans. He and Lasalle advocated taking control of government and the socializing of all property and all industry. Political methods were the most popular means taught, although there were at times sharp divergences in the preachings of Marx himself.

The continued agitation of syndicalism resulted in the declaration of the Commune of Paris in 1871. For the third time Paris was placed under the rule of the *Commune.* Probably because of this Paris has no strong city government but, like Washington, D. C, is controlled by the general government. The arguments used by the syndicalists of that day resemble very much the arguments used by Lenin when the Kerensky Government was overthrown.

Germany had just defeated France and a great indemnity had been exacted. The Communists declared that the bourgeoisie had "sold France out"; therefore they revolted. In Marseilles and other smaller cities Prince Bakounin also brought about revolts which were promptly quelled, but in Paris a large part of the National Guard joined the syndicalists and a general election was held in March at which members of the communal government were chosen. The army came from Versailles and made a strong and continuous attack. A reign of blood and terror ensued, which finally ended in the defeat of the Commune in May, twenty-five thousand communists being taken prisoners and many thousands of others deported. The leaders were executed. Thus ends the story of the revolt which was to revolutionize Europe and make all men happy.

The excuses given for this failure by the ism-ists were that Marx and Lasalle did not agree; and, that there was a conflict of interest between the workers themselves. They apparently discovered that self-interest could not be entirely eliminated.

In Germany, the continuous socialist propaganda of securing the control of government by political means gained thousands of adherents. The German people have always been firm supporters of a strong central government. They have always believed in paternalism and strict governmental regulation of all things. The sign *Verboten*, found everywhere in Germany before the great war, would, in any other country, have brought about instant denunciation.

The middle classes refused to join hands with the workers. Therefore, the socialists under the name of the Social Democratic Party went it alone. They received a serious setback because of the successful war against France and made a grave tactical error by endorsing the Paris Commune; but, in spite of these factors, at the election held in 1874 they cast more than 350,000 votes, electing nine members to the Reichstag. Three years later nearly half a million votes were cast and twelve Reichstag members elected.

Bismarck determined to destroy socialism. Two means were to be used: one, relentless repression, the other the inauguration of the well-known social welfare measures such as old-age pensions, accident insurance, old-age and invalidity insurance. The German Government became the owner of the railroads, and tobacco became state controlled and owned. The measures of repression calculated to take away the rights of the people to control and change their own government by orderly, political methods failed, as they should and ever will fail. In 1890 the Government wisely decided that it was the part of wisdom to decline to renew the statutes of persecution. This same year nearly one and one half million votes were cast for socialism and this after years of relentless Bismarckian cruelty and persecution and in spite of the fact that there was no equal suffrage.

Syndicalism, which declined after 1871, gained new strength in France in 1887 when the Council of Paris (the municipal governing body) subsidized with state money the first *bourse du travail,* or labour exchange. In reality it was in the nature of a workingmen's club where employment matters were attended to and a library furnished for the benefit of the wage workers. Immediately other cities followed the example of Paris and by 1892 there were a score of such institutions in France. The syndicalists (revolutionists) took immediate control of these centres and all who believed in direct action found a glorious opportunity to agitate, preach revolution, and foment strikes at government expense.

It was in 1892 that Aristide Briand aroused such enthusiasm at the Federation de Syndicats in Versailles that they voted a resolution endorsing the *general strike.* This had been the main bone of contention between the syndicats and the Bourse du Travail direct actionists, and this action brought about a union of the two bodies. Becoming alarmed, the Government now demanded that the old forgotten law requiring syndicats to file the names of their officers with the Government be obeyed. The organization refused. The Bourse was then raided and, by force of arms, closed. The workers, enraged, stood together for nearly a year when the conservatives who had never believed in the *general strike,* which with *sabotage* is the keystone of syndicalism, regretted their hasty action and repudiated the principle by an overwhelming vote. The revolutionaries then again took control of the Bourse du Travail and became the real, live, agitating members of that body. Disdaining political action because of the "disgraces and scandals involved," the Fédération of Syndicats virtuously decided for "direct action," particularly the general strike. Of course the fact of their hopeless minority had no influence on their decision! The Fédération stood for Proudhun-anarchy which was really group-anarchy instead of anarchy of the individual.

The following table taken from the Annuaire des Syndicats Professionels, 1911, gives the growth of revolutionary syndicalism in France:

1894	403,440 members
1896	422,777 "
1898	437,793 "
1900	491,647 "
1902	614,173 "
1904	715,576 "
1906	836,134 "
1908	957,102 "
1910	977,350 "

Of this number, but 36 per cent, belong to the Fédération or central body and at no time have half of the syndicats been united. Human nature persists in working out its future in its own way regardless of rules, fiery speeches, and glowing promises of a future of unalloyed happiness. The great organization fault of the syndicats of France has always been the irresponsibility of its membership when it actually came to paying dues. The precepts of the organization itself taught irresponsibility and more or less criminality; hence it is not strange that when the time came to pay the piper, hundreds of thousands refused. They were perfectly willing to dance but wanted someone else to pay for the music — *a basic fundamental belief* held by all syndicalists from Bakounin down to our own Haywood!

The movement has gone on in France with varying success, but always with a record of absolute defeat so far as the ultimate aims are concerned.

The characteristics of syndicats in France have always been:

Opposition to political or orderly means of any kind.

Opposition to universal suffrage.

Opposition to proportional representation.

Opposition to any form of government.

Opposition to centralized authority.

Opposition to God or religion.

Opposition to democracy.

Opposition to the rule of the majority (even among themselves).

They stand for the doctrine of force and preach it.

They stand for sabotage with all its manifest evils.

They stand for immorality and crime.

They stand for restricted production.

Their method of training: strike after strike!

Their guerrilla warfare: sabotage

Their heavy artillery: the *general strike!*

Their object: the overthrow of government and the inauguration of a dictatorship of the proletariat!

Our own I.W.W. now indorse every clause in the above statement.

The history of syndicalism shows that the proletariat are not indispensable to the rest of humanity in time of great stress, but that other men step to the front and do the work. The tying up of industry by the revolutionists has never been successful in terrifying the balance of the population for any length of time. The practice of sabotage, while irritating, has *always been more disastrous to the class that practised it than to the industry it was aimed at.* The failure of revolutionary syndicalism is but the natural outcome of such beliefs and practices. The people of the world are not cowards nor can any one *rule by fear* or achieve a good thing by bad methods. Time and again in public office one is tempted to do a little wrong that good may come; but always, when attempted, disaster follows.

The invasion of Belgium by Germany carried with it every element of cruelty and crime that devilish ingenuity could invent; but to the last the Belgians and the rest of mankind felt resentment instead of fear.

The general strike is a terrible weapon, but it is a sword with two edges. The perpetrators are invariably the ones who suffer most. The agitators, the workers who work the workers, are the only beneficiaries. Labour loses overwhelmingly, Capital but seemingly, for in the nature of things Capital makes up its loss in nine cases out of ten. True, the stoppage of production makes the whole world poorer, and no matter what the method of division may be there is *always less to divide.*

Most teachers of the isms have always looked upon wealth as an existing entity, unbounded and boundless. All their talk is of proper distribution. No one apparently paid much attention to production in Russia until Lenin found that without production increase the people of Russia would perish. Wealth is not a static thing, it changes every day; a little more production, a little more wealth; a little more consumption, a little less. It may best be stated by saying that our entire national wealth is $250,000,000,000 while our production last year amounted to about $50,000,000,000. In other words, in five years, without production, we would have no wealth left.

It is very encouraging to quote the facts of our natural resources. For instance, this country has unmined coal to the extent of 4,231,000,000 tons. This stored-up sunshine of the ages is worth absolutely nothing without labour being applied to it. It is as sandstone or salt water. Wealth is created by the application of labour to natural resources. Let all work stop and all wealth production stops. Just subtract everything that would have been produced from our wealth and you have the loss. One might just as well fire a building containing a like amount of goods — the result is absolutely the same. It is time that we all understood that restriction of production, whether by "Ca'cannie" or sabotage or cessation from work, means the same as the destruction of things already made.

The work of the revolutionists operating as syndicalists in France has had a great deal to do with the low position of France in the industrial world, and despite the thrift of its people and its many great opportunities Frenchmen have realized in small measure only their heritage. While much advance has been made it has not met the advance of the neighbouring countries of Europe. No people can escape the results of their own acts, and destruction is destruction and means loss of prosperity *no matter in what guise* destruction comes!

When a house burns down the owner collects its value from an insurance company and many people imagine there was no loss. That, of course, is a simple fallacy as someone somewhere pays for the destruction and, more than that, all the money in the world cannot replace and retrieve to the world the destroyed wealth. A friend of mine who visited France, who was by the way a great reader of John Burroughs, said: "The beautiful trees that German soldiers wantonly cut down and the orchards destroyed cut me to the heart. Twenty years of care and sometimes more are needed to replace them. The world is just that much less beautiful and that much poorer."

It were strange if, with all this agitation continuing for a century, syndicalism did not come to curse other peoples and other countries. In the next chapter we will take up syndicalism and its growth in Russia where, under the new name of bolshevism, the anarchistic communism of all the ages has become a ripened fruit, the eating thereof bringing more suffering to its people than the fabled apple in the Garden of Eden. Theories and beliefs, while oft very comforting and beautiful dreams, sometimes prove in practice to be horrible nightmares. A theory of government founded on violence, theft, sabotage, force, and wrong must in the final analysis become self-destructive and disappear or else there are no such things as *right and wrong*.

One of the salient characteristics of syndicalism is its consistent opposition to preparedness, its efforts to stop the enlisting and disciplining of an army, to check all military expenditure or preparation of any kind. The Government of France, with its neighbour Germany to the north preparing for years for war, often found itself unable to proceed as it should with preparations for its own protection. Politicians, cowardly in France as in the United States, often refused to do the right thing at the right time. The people themselves, impregnated to a certain extent with pacifism, although the danger was manifest for many long years, refused to support the Government in its preparedness endeavours. The decentralization policy of the syndicalists had its influence in the minds of the people and there never was a ready acceptance of necessary preparedness measures until the danger was right upon them. Then *it would have been too late had not the other nations of the world come to the rescue of France.*

At the time of the Franco-Prussian War, 1870-1871, the population of France was 36,102,921; of Germany 41,058,792. At the outbreak of the great conflict just terminated the population of the respective countries was: France, 39,601,509; Germany, 67,812,000.

One of the teachings which was interwoven with syndicalism was a *defiance of the laws of nature as well as the laws of man and God.* But few children were born; the reproductive duty was never taken seriously. The industrial situation was such that, strike following strike, no workman knew what the morrow would bring forth, and the result of the propaganda of selfishness and fear prevented millions from being born, and when the time came, brave and valiant as France's wonderful army was, they were too few in numbers and centralization was too new a thing for the equalling of industrial, centralized, populous Germany on the field of battle.

One hundred years of continuous advocacy of syndicalism in its revolutionary form placed France in a continually declining position industrially and it speaks much for the virility and bravery of her people that despite the handicaps of a century of anarchistic teachings, the war of self-defence rallied and united her men and women. No men at any time anywhere showed greater bravery than the far-famed poilus of France.

The constant attacks on the relations of the family could not but have their effect. The continuous preaching of anti-preparedness also bore its fruit; the demoralization of organization and the teachings of inspirational enthusiasm in place of planned and concerted effort also did its deadly work. The free-love teachings of Rousseau still remain the belief of thousands. It can be truly said that any government founded on destructive policies must fail. A government is only a collection of units. If the units are demoralized and denationalized the collection of units must be also.

A government that is continually paraded as the workmen's foe cannot evoke from the workmen that degree of self-sacrifice and loyalty necessary to succeed except under the most extraordinary circumstances.

On March 16, 1911, on the fortieth anniversary of the Commune, W. D. Haywood addressed a meeting in New York City at the Progress Assembly Rooms. With his usual carelessness as to actual facts he said that had it not been for the co-partnership of Germany and France the strikers in 1871 would have won in France, and that "they would have reestablished the great national workshops that existed in Paris and throughout France in 1848." Suppose they had done so, is there a single logical reason to believe that the result would have been one whit different than in 1848? The story of 1848 with its disaster and failure and the consequent retarding of the working-class movement carries no message to such as he, who "having ears hears not, having eyes sees not." Coleridge said:

If men could learn from history, what lessons it might teach us. But passion and party blind our eyes and the light which experience gives is a lantern on the stern which shines only on the waves behind us!

Centuries before Coleridge, Cicero rang the bell when he wrote:

Not to know what has been transacted in former times is to be always a child. If no use is made of the labours of the past ages the world must always remain in the infancy of knowledge.

No man who will read history can but regard syndicalism as silly, ineffective, useless, and cruel. Yet the same old tune played in bygone centuries pops up and for a day becomes the favourite music for those who believe in everything new, that is new to them; who believe everything true that a fanatic asserts, everything that is, wrong, and anything a better guide than experience.

It is only in government that men would imitate the crab. No one recommends the tallow dip to supplant the electric light, no one wants the ox-team to supplant the motor car, and no one wants the unwilling labour of human slaves to replace steam. In everything about us, except in plans of government, all agree that: "Each succeeding day is the scholar of that which went before it."

Chapter Eight - The Causes of Bolshevism in Russia

We deplore the outrages which accompany revolutions. But the more violent the outrages, the more assured we feel that revolution was necessary. The violence of these outrages will ever be proportioned to the ferocity and ignorance of the people; and the ferocity and ignorance of the people will be proportioned to the oppression and degradation under which they have been accustomed to live.

COULD there be a more fitting comment on Russia today than these words of Lord Macaulay's uttered many years before the Russian Revolution was dreamed of?

The Story of Russia is the story of a great, backward, good-natured child with wonderful latent talents and possibilities; undeveloped but kindly, slow to learn, ready to believe, filled with ignorant idealism and youthful enthusiasm; all kept from expression and from voice by *fear, force,* and *tyranny* made possible by the prevailing ignorance and lack of unity amongst the people themselves. So far-flung is its territory and so sparsely settled that it is no wonder that a common purpose is oft absent from amongst its people.

Think of a country with nearly three times the area of the United States — nigh one sixth the area of the earth; a country with 109,000 villages and 180,000,000 people; a country extending from the Pacific to Germany, with but a small portion of the land in use; a country that has nearly 44,000 miles as its boundary line; a country with 550,000,000 acres of forest land, the largest standing body of timber in the world. Vision a country with more than 76,000 miles of rivers, lakes, and canals, of which 17,000 are navigable for steamers; a country containing a large proportion of the most fertile land in the world; a country with a population which merely dots its surface and yet faces actual starvation every few years because of famine. Russia is neither West nor East, Oriental nor Occidental. Its government stood immovable for centuries, ignorance being the rule and not the exception, while poverty is almost universal. Its people are half men, half children. In 1903 only one thirtieth of its people were at school — in our country, one fifth were studying. Only 73 per cent, of its people can *write their own names*.

The government of the czars left Russia as their monument. The rulers demanded ignorance as an essential to their own continuance in power. Everything manmade in Russia is despicable, vile, and tyrannous — no schools, no roads, no education, no freedom, no self-rule, no prosperity, no comfort, no health. And yet nature has showered her blessings upon this land. Its soil is rich, its lakes teem with fish, its forests with game, its mountains with ore, and its people are certainly the equals, if not the superiors, of more than one European race. Can it be that without freedom and liberty even the Garden of Eden would have become an iniquitous, stinking hell-hole of unhappiness and sorrow? When you read in your morning paper of the outrages committed in Russia, pause a moment and think of the past, the past full of suffering and sorrow, ignorance and oppression, lest you judge too harshly!

As they are, so their rulers made them. The czars are dead. They should never have lived. Some day the intelligent people of the earth will realize that plague spots such as Russia cannot exist without endangering all of us. Then, and not before, will tyranny cease to be. Apparently, in 1917, the Russian people were in about the same state of development as were the people of France at the time when the "natural right of man to happiness" was taught so effectively by Rousseau. I propose to tell the pitiful story in as few words as possible, in order to help you to appreciate the reasons for the present conditions in Russia. It should be interesting, as every statement made has been carefully checked and the picture of the home environment comes firsthand from the lips of dozens of refugees who have sought asylum in our own land.

The Russian timber lands teem with game of all sorts and the production of furs, honey, wax, and resin is very large. The population, until the eleventh century, lived in stockade towns with a central fort very much the same as the outpost trading points established by the Hudson's Bay Company in our country and Canada. As in America, these trading points, chosen because of their strategical advantages, have become, in many instances, large cities.

The first great industry in Russia, as in every other country of the Old World, was dealing in human slaves.

At the time when Sverre, King of Norway, bastard child of Sigurd Mund and his cook, was instituting great reforms of every character in Scandinavia, Russia slept on and no progress for human freedom was made. When America was discovered, agriculture was just beginning in Russia. Slave labour planted the seed and slave labour reaped the harvest; but slave labour did not receive the fruits of its toil. Thus it has been in all the past centuries — the strong oppressing the weak, exploiting the helpless, waxing fat on the productive toil of others!

Commerce came first to Russia as it comes to all countries. First, the human race exploit such of the natural resources as individuals can carry away — the placer gold, the skins of animals, the honey of the wild bees, etc. The next step is usually the pastoral stage, but this never reached full development in Russia because of the fact that markets were far away and the flesh of the wild animals sufficed for the few inhabitants. The terrible winters prevented also the open range for cattle. The number of slaves became so great that the ordinary occupations incidental to commerce in primitive things could not employ them profitably; hence, the surplus human material was used in agriculture, although agriculture on an extensive scale did not come until much later. In fact, it did not come until *free peasants tilled the soil* in the fifteenth century.

It was at this time that the power of the Czar was established and the military class became the autocrats. At the same time the freedom of the peasantry was gradually taken from them. The land holdings came into fewer and fewer hands, but at the end of the sixteenth century they were still free tenants, matters being so arranged, however, that a great load of obligations to the Government and to the land owners weighed them down. They gradually became serfs of the soil, and in some matters their conditions were more wretched than those of the chattel slaves.

The Romanoff Dynasty was founded in 1613, and by 1890 Russia had become a great world power. The divergent races had become a semi-nation. The majority of the peasants were still virtually serfs and had become firmly bound to the soil.

It thus came about that a hundred years ago the population of Russia was divided into two great classes — the *land owners* and the *land tillers*. The nobility numbered less than 150,000 people. There was an inconsiderable number of preachers, doctors, lawyers, merchants, and bankers, the balance being peasants. In 1815 the Crown lands alone held 16,000,000 serfs. The great estates had two parts, one the rich and arable land set aside for the owner, the other for the workers. These workers lived in little villages called "mirs" and *paid their rent as a collective obligation or debt of the community.* The serfs were, of course, merely renters and their earnings consisted of their share of the community production, *less the rent of the landlord,* who became so rapacious that the average time they had to spend working for him in order to have the right to work for themselves reached the stupendous average of *three days per week!* Not only did he rack-rent them, but he was judge, jury, and sheriff when he desired to enforce his discipline and regulations. Under the law, no serf could leave the land where he was born. He was as much a part of the transfer, when a sale was made, as were the barns and houses, and the title that passed the land passed also *his ownership to the newcomer.* He was not even a chattel. He was real-estate, dirt!

The rubber ball thrown against the wall rebounds in the same degree as the force of the throw. The oppression and robbery and cruelty of the centuries in Russia could do no less than react in somewhat like proportion. In estimating their assets the nobles said: "We possess so many souls, not so much land." The nobility of the twentieth century in Russia reap the reward of the acts of their ancestors four hundred years before. "The iniquity of the fathers shall be visited upon the children unto the third and fourth generation."

A class which counted its wealth not in number of acres of land, but in the number of souls they possessed, can hardly expect sympathy from the world. Even Nicholas I (1828-55) admitted the peasants' wrongs and said: "Better grant some things before they take everything from us." He appointed numerous commissions which, of course, "resoluted" bravely until the land owners talked things over with them when they did nothing! Czar Alexander II, in 1857, went earnestly to work to remedy this deplorable condition. It was surely time. There were, at that time, 47,000,000 serfs in Russia. Gradually the Czar freed them on the Crown lands; and then he carried out the first and greatest little-down-and-so-much-a-year real estate deal in history. He freed the serfs and sold them the land for two and one fifth billion dollars, payable in installments running over a period of forty-nine years with interest at 6 per cent. The new owners, to be sure, had to pay whatever taxes and rates the Crown wished to impose upon them; the usual parcel, whether held in common or individually, averaging a trifle more than twenty-two acres.

Those who divided and proportioned the land were very careful to allow each family only *half enough land* to support itself. This was done in order that the great landed proprietors might have, surrounding their estates, a great mass of workers who would be compelled to work for them at whatever they wished to pay them. Despite the fact that they tilled their own holdings and worked for the neighbouring lord of the soil, famine came every two or three years to a great part of Russia, and millions lived in misery from lack of food and the essentials of life. Millions have literally died of starvation while the landed proprietors, who did nothing, lived in luxury in the capitals of Europe. An area of 550,000 square miles, or nearly one half the entire agricultural land, was disposed of in this manner. This is about eleven times the size of the state of New York and if placed in a twenty-two-mile strip would extend around the earth. "Some" real-estate deal, and this was in 1861 when folks did not think in very large figures!

It was felt that to liberate an agriculturist, without giving him ownership in land, would do no good; that landlordism was but little better than the previous condition. Government officials, apparently, were perfectly willing to protect the workers from landlord exploiters, but they only changed the yoke from a private to a governmental one; the taxes levied against the lands being greater than ever before, and as each man improved his own portion, or the portion allotted to his *mir,* the taxes immediately rose. Russia was becoming civilized and modern! The *mir,* or commune, in many instances, took title to the common lands which were cultivated, allowing the peasant ownership of only his little cot and garden.

The peasants controlled the situation, held assemblies, worked on a social and economic equality, and the head man was not the master but the *duly elected servant of the people.* It was, in fact, a village government where the practice of communism, mingled with local democracy, met with a fair measure of success. Community ownership, of course, protected *the State from the disaster that might overtake the individual owner,* thus making the collection of taxes more certain and easy; besides, it saved a vast amount of bookkeeping, and the Russians were never good accountants.

It has not been demonstrated — the late Czar, Lenin, and Trotsky to the contrary notwithstanding — that Russia is not fit for self-government. The people of Russia, by their wise choice of a constituent assembly, have shown themselves capable; and whenever a vote is taken with equal and universal suffrage in effect, no one need fear but that the people of Russia will establish a government fit to associate on equal terms with the enlightened nations of the world. The centuries of training along cooperative lines should be of immense benefit to the country when once a truly representative government comes into being.

Apparently revolutionists in every country have known that the best way to promulgate and propagate ideas is to teach their propaganda to the students in schools and universities. The mind of the student is young, easily impressed, has no personal experience by which to expose the fallacies, and there are usually no organized arguments on the other side. The teachers and professors are susceptible to ideas of this nature because of the fact that they are *always underpaid, not by a private employer but by the State;* hence, their animosity is directed against their oppressor, the State.

To a very great extent folks take their position in life from their economic situation and it were futile to expect a school teacher to feel deeply on the subject of private property when he is refused the opportunity to participate, except in a very limited degree, in that which *he is supposed to uphold and protect.* The agitators' were always aware of this and sowed the red seed among that class of people most liable and able to spread their doctrines. To be a student in Russia was to be a revolutionist! The students spread over Russia and carried the doctrines to the peasantry.

While this was going on, Alexander II inaugurated the zemstvos, which were local assemblies supposed to control schools and hospitals, teach agriculture, improve roads, etc. These were formed in 1864 and "The Reform Czar," as Alexander II was called, believed that out of these zemstvos, whose members were elected directly by the people, would come trained men fit to conduct public affairs. He looked upon them as a first step toward fitting the rank and file to participate in government. The autocrats, as might be expected, opposed every form of progress while the anarchists, of course, demanded everything at once.

In 1876 the revolutionists (revolutionary syndicalists) organized the Land and Liberty Party, which advocated the same doctrines as the French syndicalists and were practically identical with the I.W.W. of our own day. The party, of course, *taught terror as a fundamental, fear as the main doctrine, assassination as the immediate need.* Prominent government officials were chosen for the slaughter, bombs, daggers, etc., being used, but the prevailing doctrine of cowardice of the present group (I.W.W.'s) was absent. Assassins took their lives in their hands to do the deed. Many were punished. In 1880 a systematic campaign of terrorism was carried on, reaching its apex when Alexander II was killed by a bomb in March, 1881. All progress received a great set-back because of this act of violence. Many who despised the Czar and the Government and wanted real reform felt that murder could not bring about progress, and deeply resented the methods used.

However, just as soon as Alexander II was dead there was another Czar — Alexander III — who was certainly not as good a man as his predecessor. Alexander II was assassinated just at the time he had completed a *constitution for the people of Russia.* His successor, ushered in by blood, was a weak, ignorant, easily flattered idiot, who spent his time with little things and drink. For thirteen years *he was the Government,* and a mighty poor excuse for a government he was. Russia's clock of progress was turned back while the timepieces of the other countries of the world were going forward. Reaction and Divine Right to rule received continuous affirmance while the anarchists were busy gaining recruits. This Czar's main achievement was the fatherhood of the late Czar Nicholas II, a worthy scion of such a parent.

Russia was now awakening and feeling the pulse of the outside world. Our own continent was being transformed — had been transformed in fact. Railroads were being built ever5rwhere, and the transition of agricultural communities to manufacturing centres was going on apace. In 1896, the first leg of the Trans-Siberian Railroad reached the River Ob and immediately the hordes of European Russia started to emigrate for the land of promise, Siberia; the famine, with its privation and death, coming at a time to hasten colonization in Siberia. The peasants complained that they had not land enough to raise the food necessary to live. The cry was for land — tillable land — and cheap land. Land hunger has ever been the dominant factor in the shift of the populations of the earth. Access to land is the parent of emigration, oppression acting as the next greatest cause. The immense immigration to our country from Russia, especially of the Jews, explains itself when one knows their restrictions and persecutions in Russia. The chance for land and liberty will always populate the vacant places of the earth.

It is true, however, that the training received by the peasantry in the *mirs* or communistic villages deprived them of their individuality and initiative. They had never depended entirely upon themselves; hence, had little courage to pioneer a wild country. Men become strong by becoming self-dependent, and this was one of the main reasons why the people of Russia remained in crowded districts with but a small amount of land when all Siberia lay before them for colonization. Another reason, of course, was the abject poverty and ignorance of the peasantry, who knew but little of the wild land to the east and had no stored-up capital with which to maintain themselves even if they emigrated to the new country. The Russian had received herd-training and, when the time for action came, remained and functioned with the herd.

Russia from 1861 on, the date of the emancipation of the serfs, became a centre of revolutionary ferment. Partial freedom simply acted as the taste of food does to a hungry man. One must not start a people on the road to freedom unless prepared to have them go the full journey!

The Government undertook to destroy by repression the desire for liberty — executing thousands, banishing tens of thousands; but *terrorism by government is never more successful than terrorism by any other organization.* It has always been a complete failure because people (and the great war proved it again if more proof were necessary) are not afraid and cannot be made afraid. Fear of death will control only up to the point where death itself is preferable to ignoble life; after that you have a fatalist who has already discounted everything. He is then as fearless as if immortal! Absence of fear spells liberty! There were thousands of peasant revolts. The emancipation of the serfs carried with it enslavement to the State; men who lived in communes where the debt was large were not allowed to emigrate and peasants were not permitted to use the Crown lands for pasturage as theretofore.

With Russia's railroad building and industrial expansion there came to the people some degree of learning and knowledge — enough for the realization and recognition of their misery. Many left Russia for America. All wanted to leave. Returning emigrants told the story of our country and its opportunities. With the development of the manufacturing centres, principally Moscow and St. Petersburg, workmen still further assimilated syndicalism. The red seed sown by the agitators, and given firm root by the oppressors, was now carefully nurtured and propagated by the oppressed, and in the eighties along with other countries of the world, Russia had strike after strike, revolt after revolt; but all were unsuccessful. The lack of any material advance against oppression simply confined the volcano which, when the pressure became strong enough, would tear a hole in the mountain side and pour out its burning lava, destroying all live and growing things in its path.

The Social Revolutionary Party was founded in 1900, composed of peasants, workmen, and students. It was a party of communistic syndicalism, and terrorism was again its method, while assassination was practised as a cardinal principle.

We come now to the year 1905 when the war with Japan was at its height and also the time when the people of Russia were determined on securing some relief. We have seen how strike followed strike, revolt succeeded revolt, and how all disturbances although suppressed began over again the next day. The throne was tottering. It looked as though the Government must fall, as it seemed impossible that order could come again without the overthrow of Czarism.

During this time a priest named Father Gapon had gained great popularity amongst the workers. He had a strange hypnotic power which swayed the easily led Russians. In place of open revolt he advocated going to the ruler for relief. He argued that the Czar was good and only his officials were bad. He preached petition instead of demand and on January 9, 1905, clad in his priestly garments, led a procession of workers to the Winter Palace to meet and plead with the Czar for a constituent assembly based on secret, universal, equal, and direct suffrage. They wanted personal freedom, security of the person, freedom of speech and of the press, the right to assemble and the right to worship God as they saw fit; also compulsory education and free schools, equal rights before the law, an eight-hour day, normal wages, and the right to end the war by *vote of the people*. Quite a programme for the Czar to meet!

When they reached the square before the Winter Palace, troops fired into the crowds without warning, killing and wounding about 4,000 men, women, and children. This solidified the already-present desire of *all classes* to wipe out the Government. Business men, lawyers, and doctors, as well as the workmen, became a unit against oppression. Nearly all believed *The Day* had come. Murder and bloodshed had united the people against a common enemy. The Czar was "Little Father" no more, but stood out in his true colours as an oppressor of all. A free government is just as important to one class of people as to another.

The war with Japan and its failure, with the consequent depression and exposure of official incompetence and crookedness, also caused sincere and widespread desire for the overthrow of the Czar. The soldiers in the war now presented one of the most fertile fields for propaganda. Hungry, ragged, only partially armed, horribly cheated, treacherously led, they entered upon strike after strike, which were, under military law, mutinies. The sailors took possession of a man-of-war, but the Government easily prevailed and punished the mutineers. Force ruled the bodies, but the souls were still unconquered. "The body, that is but dust; the soul, it is a bud of eternity." Freedom for all is certain. Only fools doubt it and stand in its way.

After the idiotic manifestation of terrorism on the part of the Government in opening fire on the crowds before the Winter Palace, the Social Revolutionary Party, aided by thousands of new recruits, became even more frankly revolutionary and abandoned any idea of gaining help from the Government. They came to rely solely upon the only other means left to them: *force.* Sabotage had always been prevalent; now the general strike began to be advocated. With the Government's ignorance and oppression as its main ally, the general strike bade fair to bring about chaos and overthrow, at least temporarily, the Government.

In October, 1905, the Government tried to arrest and imprison the members of the Railway Congress, so called, and destroy the organization. The result was a *general strike*. Street cars stopped running; postal and telegraph employees struck; everything, even drug stores, was closed. The strike might have failed by itself but the Czar, "scared stiff," brought it to an end by a proclamation declaring a limitation of his power, affirming the principles of civil liberty, and promising that no law should become effective without the sanction, consent, and support of the Duma or national assembly. In plain words, he proposed to inaugurate a constitutional government in Russia and on October 17, 1905, issued his manifesto which, stripped of its introductory verbiage, reads:

We make it the duty of the Government to execute our firm will:

(1) To grant the people the unshakable foundations of civic freedom on the basis of real personal inviolability, freedom of conscience, of speech, of assemblage, of unions.

(2) To admit now to participation in the Imperial Duma, without stopping the pending elections and in so far as it is feasible in the short time remaining before the convening of the Duma, all the classes of the population, leaving the further development of the principle of universal suffrage to the new legislative order.

(3) To establish as an unshakable rule that no law can become binding without the consent of the Imperial Duma, and that the representatives of the people must be guaranteed a real participation in the control over the lawfulness of the authorities appointed by us.

He granted, as a matter of fact, an imperial consent which might be revoked at any time. He still was Czar and autocrat; for a time a more reasonable one 'tis true, but still autocrat. He still claimed the right to interpret his promises and break them if he saw fit. How slow the old order dieth! If a man is told often enough and long enough that he is a great man, chosen of God to rule, he comes to believe it, unless he has a sense of humour. This the tyrants always lack. They never laugh at themselves; laughter cures bigotry. The futility of granting, during or after a battle, those things which should have been given without the asking, has no better example than the story of Russia. When will men learn to forestall defeat by doing the right thing at once." The reason measures of reform failed in Russia was that there was no intent of true reform. The thread of Czarism, or autocracy, distrust of the people, flouting their just grievances, laughing at their weaknesses, sneering at their sufferings, and *always refusing them real power* — imperial anarchy in other words — runs through every promise and every proclamation!

But the harvest day for the rulers had come; the grain was fast ripening and no human power could stay its fruition. As well try to halt the sun in its course through the heavens! The Czar and his sycophants, however, saw only the surface of the great, slow mass-movement. They did not want to understand and feared even to think the truth. The people — stolid, patient, silent — bided their time. Cruelty was accentuated; repression made still stronger; more rights were taken away; the franchise was limited mostly to the landed gentry; the bureaucratic system made its evils felt daily; the country was placed under martial law, and all principles of civil liberty were violated.

Chapter Nine - The Czar and the Duma Come to the Parting of the Ways

A WRONG thing can never stand the light of day. The Duma, though weak and inefficient, did one thing — it turned on the sun's rays and Russia finally emerged from isolation and darkness and entered a phase of twilight they called representative democracy. It was not a representative democracy. All legal, orderly methods had failed because of military oppression, and like every people in such circumstances, the Russians embraced syndicalism, direct action, sabotage, general strike, and revolution. This seemed to be their only possible escape, their only possible means of gaining freedom. They felt they must overcome force with a greater force.

Force never does any real good in the world of ideas! The only people who obey force are those who preach and practise it. "He that killeth with the sword must be killed with the sword." (Rev. xlii-10.)

Before you blame the courageous souls who revolted in Russia, however, ask yourself what you would have done had you been there. I am sure I would have tried to bring freedom to Russia had I been a Russian, and feel certain that you would have done the same. One can excuse the excesses of the helpless! Revolutions will continue to occur wherever tyranny is practised, wherever robbery is permitted, wherever equal rights are denied, wherever there is no other method of effective expression of the soul of mankind. Oppression brings its own antidote! Injustice is but temporary — justice is eternal!

If mankind, inherently, has a natural right, it is the right of equality before the law. Denied, chaos must come; granted, things right themselves, though mayhap through travail and suffering. People are not only fit to govern, but must govern. Otherwise, there is no peace, no security, and no real government! Better no government for a time than a government so brutal that it will listen to no argument but violence!

In gaining the proper perspective of conditions that brought about the upheaval in Russia, it were well to pause for a moment and consider the conditions of life of the great mass of the Russian people. Before we breathe one word of condemnation it is but fair to put ourselves in their places. How did the masses live? What hope for relief had they? What hope for their future?

Briefly sketched, their history reveals a past so dark, so gruesome, so bereft of liberty and light, of freedom and opportunity, that its recitation cannot fail to cause every sincere lover of freedom to take the side of these oppressed and exploited people. Picture to yourself a nation of millions, a small number living in towns and cities, the majority huddled together in one hundred and nine thousand mud-thatched, straw-roofed village huts; each *mir*, village, or commune having about half as much land to till as *was sufficient to maintain even the simple Russian scale of living.* To this picture must be added a visitation of *famine* every two or three years with its consequent suffering and death. Vision a government whose sole aim is to maintain itself at the expense of every one of these millions and you have a meagre idea of the conditions under which the great majority of these people were forced to live.

One third of the population were non-Russian: Letts, Lithuanians, Poles, Finns, Jews, etc. Every branch of the Government used every known device to inflame the Russians against those of alien blood. It made no difference that they had lived on the land for centuries, no matter that they had supported the Crown by their taxes and their toil; in fact, nothing mattered except that the *Czar keep his tyrannous crew afloat.* The blood of a few hundreds of thousands mattered not. Hatred of all other races was taught, preached, and practised, while the secret police were subsidized to inject the virus of hatred and suspicion between men. The Czar had no dangerous external enemy. He manufactured one even more potent: an internal enemy — the alien races — and the product of his manufacture, his creation, was helpless.

Religious and racial differences brought about internal dissensions. Encouraged by the Government, sometimes instigated and protected by it, massacre after massacre took place. The murderers were rewarded while those who denounced them were imprisoned, banished, or killed. Russia's subject races have so suffered for centuries. The Jews were permitted to live in only half the towns. All Jewish schools were to be closed and the race of Abraham was not to be allowed to secure any education, anywhere. When things were reasonably quiet the Government, through its agents, sold the Jews privileges, but when trouble came to the throne, the Jews were arrested, imprisoned, robbed, and killed. They were given the right to sell liquor; then the law was repealed, again granted, and again the privilege was repealed. The laws forbade them to deal in land — it was repealed, then enacted again and enforced or not enforced, as the agents saw fit — and then it became absolute law. Certain districts were laid off within which the Jews could live, called the "pale"; outside of these districts Jews were forbidden. Although the Jewish population increased the rulers saw to it that the size of these districts was diminished, resulting in squalor, overcrowding, dirt, filth, and disease. The Jews were also shut out from agriculture, and thus forced to become small tradesmen and dealers, and because of this land policy of the Czar it was easy to shift the blame to the Jews when famine came to curse the country.

By their thrift and trading with the peasantry they accumulated money and became the country's petty capitalists. As such, they were blamed for all the ills of the poor. Ignorant, hungry, starving, the villagers periodically attacked them, stole their goods, murdered their families, and burned their homes.

The Government, as might be expected, kept the progressive and profitable businesses for itself, taking governmental control of many staples and charging the consumer oft-times three to four times as much as the same articles were sold for in neighbouring countries. The money so derived was used, not for the benefit of the country, but for benefiting and enriching the nobility. In one of the richest countries of the earth there was no escape for the great majority from poverty and want! Compulsory poverty and pre-determined ignorance ruled in every hut in Russia!

Not satisfied with these and other monopolies, high protective duties were placed on articles of general use. Indirect taxes were piled heap upon heap. When the peasantry began using tea, sugar, and steel plows, taxes were again increased, the starving people of Russia paying three to four times as much for such articles as the peoples of France and Germany. So expensive are steel implements that harrows, plows, and wagons are made of wood. Tea is only an occasional drink, while the use of sugar is very limited. In a starving country, the very farmers, although suffering for lack of food, *were compelled by need to sell their grain for export.* Ninety-seven per cent, of the exports of Russia were for years and years *raw material.* Sixty-six per cent, of the exports from starving Russia is grain, only 3 per cent, being manufactured articles. While the peasantry were starving, the landowners and nobles were loaned money by the State at very much less than the current rates of interest. Surely a government *by the few, and for the few!*

Count Witte admitted that the condition of the farmers was one hundred years behind the times. Conditions of agriculture were primitive, the peasants getting but about one third as much produce per acre as the Germans, despite the fact that the soil of Russia comprises the best in the world. Russia has always been incredibly poor, the peasants never getting enough ahead to take advantage of modern methods or machinery. The Government was not even wise enough to follow the example of the former slave owners. The Government knew the value of modernity in industry and farming; they knew that a well-fed man would do the work of three "underfeds," and yet they saw to it that the peasants were undernourished. They knew that the ignorant are always inefficient and poor producers; still they planned for continuous and never-ending ignorance.

They were fools! A fool in power is more dangerous than a knave! The land allotted was insufficient to support the people while at the same time the compulsory poverty and ignorance of the people themselves held down the productiveness of the land they had.

The people, however, had their own ideas of right and wrong. They refused, times without number, to allow the Czar to dictate to them as to their village business, and refused to recognize their village head as a little czar —

he was always treated as their servant. The land was divided between the villagers by themselves and redistributed every three years, the result being that no individual had any incentive to enrich or fertilize his portion of the public domain; therefore the land became poorer year by year. The peasantry simply mined the land, but did not farm it.

The Czar tried many times to overthrow village rule, but against the resistance of the peasantry he found himself helpless. It was the old story of the patient man submitting to every wrong until the usurper entered into his family arrangements. Further interference spelt immediate revolt. The Czar had his choice of allowing the democracy of the villages to continue, or seeing the *whole country become free*. To hold his job, he submitted time and again, but in revengeful retaliation tried to shut out all light, information, and intelligence from the villages. Education was taboo; books were prohibited; newspapers, pamphlets, etc., had to be circulated in secrecy. There were few railroads, no good roads, no privacy in the mails, and *all who travelled were under suspicion.* There were few isolated farmhouses, virtually all tillers of the soil living in villages. Their sons sometimes went to the large centres to learn to read and think. To remember is an inherited faculty and needs no training. And such memories! A sister violated, a babe starving, a midnight attack, murder, homes in flames, Siberia, prison, death! Oh, the memories! Well might the potentate tremble in his palace! The accumulated resentment of the centuries must fall upon his head. Someone has said:

There is a spirit of resistance implanted by God in the breast of man proportioned to the size of the wrongs he is destined to endure.

The Russians were not only poor — they were paupers. Even the windmills were owned in common, while the flocks of sheep and cattle were so few that one lone child could tend the entire possessions of a village. Surrounding each village was a stockade and one could neither leave nor enter without first reporting to the authorities. The huts were plastered inside and out with mud and thatched with grasses and straw. Each hut had but a single door and two rooms — its size 15 by 30 feet. The cattle, pigs, chickens, etc., were kept in the entrance room, the family and boarders living in the inside chamber. The whole family group, a dozen or more, herded together under unspeakable conditions. In many parts of Russia wood is scarce. If you open the door for air, this means fuel. Fuel costs money, labour, effort — aye, more, it means less food for the hungry — hence, no open doors or windows. The smell of the cattle and swine, the odour of crowded humanity, the crowding together of both sexes in a little room, some of whom were not even relatives — vision the picture and imagine the result yourself. The furniture — a table, a bench or shelf around the wall, the top of the Russian stove reserved as a sleeping place for the old. They eat, sleep, breed, are born and die in this room!

The health conditions are unbelievable. Syphilis has become a terrible scourge in Russia. According to the American Social Hygiene Association,

"Sixty per cent, of syphilis in Russia is acquired through lack of decent living conditions and a gross ignorance of personal hygiene. The disease has largely lost its characteristics as a sexual disease, because it is so generally contracted outside of sexual relations. In some villages every man, woman, and child is infected."

In describing how widespread the scourge has become in Russia, Vedder in his work on "Syphilis and Public Health" says:

In the Parafiew District, consisting of six villages with a population of 9,500, only about 5 per cent, of the people are not syphilitic.

My experience as mayor of Seattle, when I had supervision of the quarantine of several hundred diseased men and women, gives me full realization of the effect this disease must have in Russia. Even under the most approved, scientific, and modern treatment administered under the supervision of Dr. J. S. McBride, as Commissioner of Health of the city of Seattle, the effects of the disease were only too apparent. In many instances, paresis, locomotor ataxia, and feeble-mindedness developed despite the best of care and treatment. We found that in practically every instance the disease had destroyed most of the attributes of the manhood or womanhood as well as the moral fibre of the patient!

The terrible effects of this disease raging rampant throughout Russia can hardly be imagined. It surely has left its impress on the moral, mental, and physical condition of the Russian people. Smallpox is so prevalent in Russia that one seldom meets, in Seattle, an emigrant from that country who does not bear its marks on his countenance. Infectious and contagious diseases have unrestricted range, as quarantine regulations, etc., are practically unknown.

The clothing worn by the Russian peasants is of the cheapest and apparently is never discarded. The average Russian farmer not only has too few clothes for comfort, but too few for decency. His food consists in the main of bread and potato soup; his vegetables — green cucumbers, sometimes a watermelon; his beverage — a drink made from sour bread, with tea once in a great while, sometimes a little sugar, while meat is a rarity in a country wonderfully adapted to grazing! The privilege of picking berries or killing wild game was denied them, and straw was mixed with their flour to make it more bulky.

Does any one wonder that Russia was seething with revolution? Remember that the women worked in the fields even harder than the men and prepared the sparse meals as well. Children were often born in the fields, but in a period of three or four days the women were again at their toil. I am informed that, as a result, most Russian women are far from well. The death rate is double that of most backward countries. Infants die by the thousands from lack of nutrition while many of those that survive are undersized.

The ordinary peasant earned, or rather *received,* about one fourth the income of the French peasant. In many villages the average family income was less than $75.00 per year, half of which went for taxes, direct or indirect. When famine came, the milch cows and other livestock must either starve to death or be sold. They were usually mortgaged, the money going to the money lender. Each succeeding year sees the community just that much more unfit for the struggle. And while the people starved the export of grain continued. The year 1906, a famine year, showed an actual increase in the export of food products. While we, in this country, were bitterly complaining of hard times in 1907, nearly one hundred million people in Russia were facing death through starvation.

Ten years ago economists of note calculated that with the same efforts at cultivation as exist in the United States, Russia could support a population of two hundred and fifty million people in comfort and decency. To-day, the figures must be increased at least 50 per cent, on account of the superior equipment and modern improvements which have been inaugurated since that time.

Not only is the peasant unable to raise enough food to feed himself from the land allotted him, but with the help of his labour sold to the big holders of land near the village he is still in the circumstances depicted — a pauper on the verge of starvation every second or third year.

To any one who may question my facts in relation to Russia I desire to say that I have talked with dozens of men from villages all over Russia, who, by some miracle, escaped thraldom and came to the United States. Not only is the story here told not exaggerated, but it is literally discounted and understated. No man in America could be made to believe the truth without actually visioning the misery, poverty, and degradation that the Government of the czars brought to the Russian people.

Schools there were none, or practically none. Education was as much restricted to the cities as the supplying of gas. Ignorance prevailed everywhere. Only the revolutionists taught the people anything. To these villagers came the socialist, the anarchist, the syndicalist and the bolshevist! No wonder they were welcomed! Revolutionists brought them dreams of a paradise on earth, dreams of a country without landlords, dreams of plenty, dreams of peace, dreams of clothing, dreams of an education for the children, dreams of rest and comfort and happiness and peace. Welcome? Of course they were welcome, thrice welcome! Listen? Of course they listened. Believed? Yes, they believed. Go to any jail and say to the prisoners: "If you all do this to-morrow or the day after, you will be free!" Try it! You will find that even the deaf will hear and understand!

I have no quarrel with men demanding freedom and liberty and equal rights. I love such men and so do you. I have no quarrel with the revolutionists of Russia. Wendell Phillips said:

Revolutions are not made, they come. A revolution is as natural a growth as an oak. It comes out of the past. Its foundations are laid far back.

My quarrel is with the men who, after the people had secured control of the

Government and stood ready to elect a constituent assembly by secret, equal, and universal suffrage, overthrew the people's Government by force, by means of a small militant minority, and instituted a government *of the few, by the few, and for the few!*

The darkest page in the history of the world is not the blood-stained story of the czars, though God knows that is bad enough; it is not the story of the Sultan of Turkey; it is not the story of the rule of any czars or kings or emperors — but it is the story of the betrayal of the great Russian people by Lenin, the greatest hangman in history, and his autocratic, czar-imitating brethren.

Here was a great, patient people, silent and longsuffering, with centuries of sorrow and want and poverty ingrained in their very souls; their brains darkened by oppression; stunted, half of the East, half of the West, half man, half child; and at last, through untold sacrifice, opportunity comes — freedom, self-government, is in their grasp; a constituent assembly is to be chosen, universal suffrage has been gained, everything is ready for the world's greatest experiment — and then, a few ne'er-do-wells, a few fanatics, a few scoundrels, who had claimed for years to be friends of liberty, tear the cup from their lips, steal their hardly won freedom, institute a reign of czarism turned upside down, make slaves of the people, and *betray those who trusted them!*

Judas betrayed his Saviour, Benedict Arnold betrayed military secrets, but Lenin and Trotsky and the bolshevists betrayed one hundred and eighty million free people, and by assassination and force drove them back into slavery. History will condemn the Czar, but he was supporting his creed and his class; the leaders of Germany plunged the world into war, but Lenin and Trotsky betrayed their own blood-brothers into slavery and took the positions of slave drivers and executioners for themselves! The ox that heads his fellows under the killing-hammer in the Chicago stockyards is a God by comparison! Murderers of men have ever been execrated by mankind, but how much more will future generations in Russia despise these men who, with words of friendship and love on their lips, stole a people's birthright and murdered the hope and happiness of millions?

The Duma was dissolved because it asked the Czar to observe his own proclamation. In this manifesto he said, as you will recall:

We obligate the Government to fulfill our *unchangeable* will as follows: 1st, The population is to be given the inviolable foundation of civil rights based on the inviolability of the person, freedom of belief, of speech, of organization and meeting...The working out of the principle of universal suffrage will be left to the new legislative body...No law can be put into effect without the consent of the Duma.

On the tenth day of March, 1906, the Czar convoked the legislative assembly but no legislative work was accomplished. The Czar simply wanted a consultative assembly, while the Duma wanted to be the whole government. The

Czar's friends had, in the meantime, started a series of the worst massacres in the history of Russia. The Duma demanded control of the officials of the Government and punishment of the guilty leaders. The Czar dissolved the Duma. A typically Russian situation!

The Second Duma was convened, but its only law worthy of mention was the Electoral Law. After the dissolution of the Second Duma, the Czar by decree modified this law. The Encyclopaedia Britannica says in relation to the acts of the First and Second Dumas:

As for the revolutionary "intellectuals" without the level of agrarian discontent, they were practically powerless, the more so as their political activity consisted mainly in "building theories for an imaginary world." The bourgeois revolutionists of France had all been philosophers, but their philosophy had at least paid lip-service to "reason," the Russian revolutionists who formed the majority of the First and Second Dumas, as though inspired by the exalted nonsense preached by Tolstoi, subordinated reason to sentiment until — their impracticable temper having been advertised to all the world — it became easy for the Government to treat them as a mere excrescence on the national life, a malignant growth to be removed by a necessary operation.

Apparently, the get-it-all-at-once crowd demanded too much and got nothing!

The Third Duma came into being December 14, 1907, and lasted nine years. As a result of the restrictions on the right of suffrage, it was composed of landlords and supporters of the Czar. The people saw through the transparent evasion of the promises of the Czar, but the time came when even this assembly, handpicked as it was, fought with courage against the Czar himself. A few reforms were inaugurated, but the time for gradual change had passed. Naught but a cataclysm would satisfy the repressed millions. It was in vain that the Government enacted legislation tending to assist the modernization of Russia. The people had lost faith in their rulers. Everyone, except an infinitesimal few, wanted czarism wiped off the earth.

John Spargo in his book "Bolshevism" says:

The period 1906-14 was full of despair for sensitive and aspiring souls. The steady and rapid rise in the suicide rate bore grim and eloquent testimony to the character of those years of dark repression. The number of suicides in St. Petersburg increased during the period 1905-09 more than 400 per cent.; in Moscow, about 800 per cent. In the latter city two fifths of the suicides in 1908 were of persons less than twenty years old!

Czarism maintained itself by employing the armed forces of the empire against the helpless and unarmed people. Those who could, sought asylum in foreign lands. In 1901, 85,000 Russians came to the United States; in 1907, 259,000, and in 1913, 295,000. Of the 3,300,000 immigrants who have come to the United States from Russia during the past century, 2,500,000 came during the period 1900 to 1914.

Our country has about twice the population per square mile that Russia has and yet the people of Russia come to a country twice as crowded because our Government is a free government under which every man and woman has equal rights. No better commentary on the value and worth of our institutions could be given.

You will note that 75 per cent, of the emigrants from Russia to the United States came here after the desire and need of freedom and liberty had become apparent to them. The more one considers the idiotic rule of the late Czar and his cohorts and the length of time they were able to control the destinies of the Russian people, the less one believes in the near-at-hand establishment of a government in Russia based upon freedom, liberty, and equal rights for all.

These people allowed themselves to be kept in subjection by a very ordinary, ignorant, feeble product of the most corrupt court in Christendom. He was not even a strong despot, being helpless when pitted against his nobles or his German wife. He canonized a monk who had been dead for half a century, believing that he had successfully pleaded with God to send him a male heir. He refused to learn from the story of the past; used his full power to befog the lessons of the present, and apparently believed that upon the structure of violence and tyranny he would be able to control the future! Poor fool!

"Whatsoever a man soweth, that shall he also reap." (Gals. vi-7.) The ruling powers of Russia had shoved all their chips into the centre of the table; they had drawn all the cards they could draw; their hand was but a "fourflush." The only question was when the people would call their bluff. Called — they knew they must lay down their hand and retire! Nothing but a fight, with the consequent breaking up of the game, could put off the end!

And that is exactly what occurred.

Chapter Ten - How the World War Saved, the Revolution Destroyed, and Lenin Reestablished, Czarism

IN JUNE, 1914, I was in the office of the *Spokesman Review* in Spokane. The telegrapher lazily turned around and announced that a prince, whose name he could not quite make out, had been assassinated at Sarajevo, the capital of Bosnia. The office force yawned and went on with their work. The editor and myself hardly checked our conversation. A prince more or less, what did it really amount to anyway? It was so far away — and yet, the death of a man on the other side of the earth was all the spark needed to bring about a world conflagration. War was declared.

Russia came to life. The wavering fortunes of czarism seemed to receive new life. The country became an armed camp. Temple bells tolled in the one hundred and nine thousand villages; priests gathered their flocks; peasants and workers and landlords alike became, for the time being, one — with but a single thought apparently, and that thought the protection of the frontiers of Russia. All the people knew was that war with Germany was on. Where the war was, how far away, what kind of people were at war, few knew.

The soldiers gathered while the officials began to wind and unwind red tape. Certain preparations were made. Money was poured out like water; factories producing railroad supplies, etc., began to turn out, or try to turn out, guns; no provision being made, however, for the industrial necessities of a long war. No one thought it would last for any length of time. Russia was face to face with her ancient enemy, Germany. It looked as though war would cement the hostile factions. The leading men in court circles were Germans; the Czarina was a German princess; many of the military leaders were also German, and as we look backward, one cannot help but believe that the preparations were insincere and were purposely held back and made inefficiently.

Millions joined the army. The peasantry, untrained and only partially armed, always half-starved and miserably led, obeyed orders, and their lives were the sacrifice offered on the altar by the Czar.

Armies in the front trenches had but one gun for two and sometimes four soldiers. The unarmed waited until the armed were killed and then grasped the rifles from the dying. If an officer showed ability, he was sent back into interior villages where he could give no help. The defeated generals were promoted; the successful ones demoted. The weakest battalions were placed in trying positions; those of experience were bivouacked miles from the front. The wholesale murder by the efficient Germans at the front was materially aided by the pro-Germans in the rear.

Box cars were sent empty from Vladivostok to Petrograd to get their numbers painted, then sent back again empty, across half the earth, to receive a load. There was little organization, no real spirit. Incompetence and criminal negligence were the rule — not the exception. And yet the soldiers, dumb, patient, brave, fought to the death. The swamps of the Mazurian Lakes, the drive into Galicia, the battles in the ice and snow, all alike proved the natural courage of the soldiers and the lack of ability and the criminal conspiracy of the leaders. It was a nightmare of blood and murder; of useless sacrifice and bravery; of death and sorrow! A human life was held at less than a sack of wheat and men were punished by standing them unarmed in the front lines under the fire of the German machine guns. It was a most brutal exhibition of ruthlessness by the rulers, not against another people, but against their own flesh and blood.

The Russian soldiery fought bravely, but when the efficient German murder machine really got under way, defeat followed defeat, retreat succeeded retreat, and hundreds and thousands of falsely led, poorly armed, and half-starved Russians were killed; millions of others were in open revolt. The people back home knew that their brothers were being slaughtered — knew that the officers were fighting for Germany and not for Russia, and they demanded a reform in military affairs. No such reform, however, was forthcoming. The rulers had *unprepared* too well.

By 1917, defeat appeared certain. Strike after strike took place, culminating in a general strike as a protest against the unfairness shown in the distribution of food. The people believed there was enough bread if it was properly and fairly distributed. The soldiery stood with the people.

Revolution began on March 10, 1917. The Czar or his underlings had planned too well the defeat of Russia. In accomplishing it they destroyed the officers, *who came almost entirely from the ranks of the nobility and the richer classes.* The result was that new officers and line soldiers who came direct from the oppressed people became the leaders, the thinkers, the doers; and when the Government was attacked, these men *with the memories of centuries of oppression burned into their very souls, turned their rifles and persuaded their soldiers to fight against the ruling class and not against their own brethren.* Such was the result of czarism; such the well-earned reward that autocracy and oppression always receive under like circumstances!

On March 12, 1917, the famous Preprazkensky regiment refused to fire on the revolutionary crowds, and mutinied. Other soldiers who were brought up to suppress the insurrection took the side of the revolutionists. Practically all the regiments quartered in Petrograd assisted joyfully in the Government's overthrow. Other soldiers were called from the front, but those who had already taken sides with the people fraternized with them and won their support.

On March 17, 1917, the Czar said he had had enough and the Duma instituted a provisional government, Kerensky being named Minister of Justice and Gutchokoff Minister of War.

Czarism was overthrown, as it should have been overthrown centuries before. Russia was ready for a representative form of government at least a century before the revolution. Had it been granted, Russia to-day would be in the forefront of human society; denied, as it was, the people went to extremes in exact proportion to their repression.

Gutchokoff soon resigned, because the self-appointed Council of Workmen and Soldiers' Deputies had demanded the right to vise his orders. Kerensky then became Minister of War. Among his first orders he issued a *decree abolishing the death penalty in the army.* This completely demoralized the army and it gradually became an unorganized, unled mob. The German propagandists circulated forged newspapers and pamphlets among the peasant soldiery, telling them that the land back home was being divided and the Government wanted them to hurry home so they could get their share. They threw away their arms, oft-times killed their officers, and started for home. The army became a rabble!

Kerensky, the people's idol, became the head of the Government. Universal suffrage and the right of representation had come to the people of Russia. An election was called to choose members of a constituent assembly. All men and all women could vote. Russia was free, but the people did not understand the difference between *liberty* and *license.* The jump from ruthless repression to liberty came so quickly that they were dazed.

The Czar's regime had forced the Russian people into but two classes — the very rich and the very poor, the poor outnumbering the rich many fold. There was but a very small middle class and they, almost to a man, aided the poor in their fight for freedom.

Of course, the people expected from the new Government more than any government could do. The assembly to be elected must be truly representative of all Russia. Few realized that a government is necessarily a pauper and lives only by the contributions of the people. Few knew that happiness and prosperity must come from service and work and not from the mere passing of resolutions.

What an opportunity for the Lenins and Trotskys to assist in the formation of a truly representative government! What a chance to show vision and breadth and world bigness! The people, held so long in darkness and sleep, suddenly awoke. They expected everything — Utopia by wireless, food by law, education by immediate absorption, crops without planting, sustenance without toil! Liberty, to them, meant license — wealth, simply for the taking. The golden opportunity for the men who had fought against autocracy was now at hand. They could have assisted Kerensky, could have explained the manifold difficulties, could have counselled patience and love, instead of hurry and hate, but they did no such thing.

From the prisons of Siberia came the thousands of political exiles who, in their youth, had embraced the fantastic doctrines of anarchy. In prison they did not progress, or learn by bitter experience that human nature has its limitations and frailties. They came from Siberia teaching the untried, and, in fact, exploded doctrines of their youthful enthusiasm, beginning in the same state of mind as when exiled. All government meant to them was persecution, wrong, force, violence.

Nikolai Lenin was, at the time, in Switzerland. The German Government furnished him with a special train across Germany in order that he might enter Russia and assist in the overthrow of Kerensky which Germany deemed essential to its cause, as one of the first acts of the Kerensky Government was to pledge Russia's allegiance to the cause of the Allies and to the continuance of the war against Germany. Money was furnished him and such as he in unlimited quantities and every aid was given him both by the monarchical party in Russia and by the rulers of Germany, in order that he might successfully combat the establishment of a constitutional government in Russia.

They had picked their man well. Lenin was unscrupulous and determined to establish a bolshevist or syndicalist form of government. The monarchists believed that if they could establish a dictatorship under their friend Lenin, they would be able to overthrow such a form of government at any time they chose and reestablish czarism once more in Russia. For centuries the German plan had been to keep Russia in a backward economic condition. They wanted Russia to continue furnishing an ever-increasing supply of raw material for their factories, whose product was to be sold in turn to unprogressive, non-industrial Russia. If Russia became an industrial nation they believed she would be Germany's greatest trade rival. Russia free meant poverty for Germany, they thought.

Lenin never denied having received German gold. His apologists say that he would have accepted bribes from any one for use in furthering his propaganda and that while apparently serving Germany he planned all the time to cheat Germany of the fruits of its bribes by continuing the Bolshevist Government indefinitely.

From every part of the world came other dreamers, adventurers, criminals — filled to the Adam's apple with book-taught panaceas and selfish purposes — all wanting to get home to Russia and get home quick in order to try their individual plan, their scheme!

Russia was like a patient brought to a clinic of uneducated and inexperienced surgeons, with plenty of knives to cut with but with no healing ointments. All diagnosed the case differently. All wanted to operate on different parts of the patient. Disagreements, recriminations, hatred, were the order of the day. From our own shores the refugee anarchists who had sought shelter in America returned. Trotsky tried to get back. Our Government for a time refused him passports until Kerensky himself, believing in the reasonableness of mankind, asked our Government to allow Trotsky's return, in order that he might help him and help Russia. We said "all right" and Trotsky and a hundred thousand others like him returned home to try out their street-corner theories of no government. The present Russian Government may well be said to be that of *the soap-boxers of the world*.

Upon their return to Russia they immediately began an organized attempt to overthrow majority rule. Those who had never been able properly to conduct a peanut stand advocated that they be placed in charge of two hundred million people! The dregs of the world gathered and demanded that they be made autocrats! Loud-voiced, plausible, full of the catch phrases of class hatred, they found a ready response among many, but well they knew that the Russian peasant stood not for anarchy but order, decency, and a stable, centralized government. They believed they were especially anointed to rule' the ignorant. They felt the people were not fit to rule. They were to be the chosen shepherds of the flock, and if the flock did not appreciate these self-chosen place seekers, it was the flock's fault and not the shepherds'! They preached free speech, free press, equal pay, confiscation of all wealth, death to the intelligent, plenty of rest, lots of food, and everything else that might gain support, and still they remained in a hopeless minority.

There was but one course left for these agitators. They would overthrow the Government; they would have a counter revolution; they would gain control of the food and ammunition supplies in Petrograd and *then* they would seize the reins of power and inaugurate a dream government from which all blessings would flow. They talked not of production, but of division; not of producing food, but of eating it; not of making clothes, but of wearing them; not of labour, but of rest.

Kerensky, apparently, did not realize that there can be no compromise between government and men who hate all government; that there can be no common meeting ground between law and order and anarchy; that kindness and conciliation are not only wasted effort, but are absolutely dangerous when your opponents are enemies of all law and order. He talked and wrote and preached and did everything but use the only weapon anarchists understand, which is *force — and plenty of it!*

Whenever any one tries to usurp authority, the officials have but one duty to perform, and that is, obey their oath. *A government that will not defend itself cannot stand!* Minority rule is based *per se* on the proposition that the majority are too ignorant to rule. Kerensky faltered and altered, pleaded and then threatened. He tried the impossible and failed. Hesitating to shed blood, his hesitation caused the murder of innocent thousands; refusing to imprison the bad, he lived to see the good and innocent jailed! With sickly sentimentality as his watchword and vague speeches for his edged tool, he saw a small militant band of adolescent "intellectuals" seize control of a government which he had not the courage to protect!

Our ambassador to Russia, David R. Francis, says that Kerensky made his fatal mistake when he did not use force to destroy the power and influence of the bolshevists at an uprising on the third and fourth of July, 1917. He felt that Kerensky should have imprisoned Lenin and Trotsky at this time and punished them as traitors to the country.

If the same red blood had coursed through the body of Kerensky that pulsed through the veins of Theodore Roosevelt, Russia to-day would be a free, self-governing republic, immune by its immensity from any foreign foe and protected from great internal troubles by the freedom granted to the people. His weakness, however, does not excuse the betrayers of Russia. On every street corner in the world, in millions of pamphlets, they had declaimed for freedom, liberty, and equal rights, for a government of love and not of force, for free speech, free press, etc.

Lenin and Trotsky, with *made-in-Germany* propaganda, planned to be *The Government.* Make no mistake about that! Lenin knew what he wanted, and believing in *direct action,* if opportunity offered, would take it. With no moral scruples or conscience to check him, he determined to try, once more, the exploded doctrines of syndicalism. Poor Russia was to be the patient and Germany the gainer, no matter what happened.

Three weeks before the Constituent Assembly was to be elected Kerensky's Government was overthrown by a militant minority and a reign of arson, murder, force, violence, repression, hatred, and theft took its place. A dictatorship of the proletariat was announced and Lenin became the Dictator.

Kerensky ran away.

What Bolshevism Did

The election for the Constituent Assembly had been called for November twenty-fifth. Lenin and the bolshevists at first believed that they would be able to win at the polls; hence, they spoke in favour of the Assembly, but as election day drew near they sensed that they were in a hopeless minority and began to talk of the ignorance of the masses and adopted repressive measures in order that the bolshevist side might win. They were against universal suffrage, but felt they were not strong enough to stop the holding of the election.

They used Mexican political methods, including all means of suppression and the use of governmental influence, but when election day rolled around, thirty-six million free men and women of Russia went to the polls and chose their representatives to meet on December twelfth and establish a stable government by adopting a constitution and laws for all Russia. Less than two hundred thousand bolshevist votes were cast out of the thirty-six million.

Lenin and Trotsky found themselves in a hopeless minority. It was certain that the Constituent Assembly would adopt a constitution and laws which would drive them from power. It was certain that a government of the majority would be established and that, under majority rule, the dictatorship of Lenin and Trotsky would cease. The elected members were to meet December 12, 1917. On December eleventh the Cadets (Constitutional Democrats) who were in Petrograd were arrested by order of Lenin, as counter-revolutionists. Many others went into hiding, afraid to appear at the appointed meeting place. The *Government of the Soap Boxers* refused to permit the meeting of the popularly elected representatives of the people.

On January eighteenth, with 423 members present, the Constituent Assembly finally attempted to hold a meeting. A great many members had been terrorized and driven away by fear of imprisonment and death. Lenin believed that he and his could control and manipulate the balance for their own purposes. Ambassador Francis says: "There was a great demonstration in Petrograd on the part of the people to manifest their joy on the assembling of a constituent assembly." The bolshevists were in the minority in the Assembly notwithstanding the Cadets had not come and some of the social revolutionists of the Right (Moderates) were not present.

But when the first vote was taken for election of officers, despite the armed forces of the Reds which surrounded the building and filled the corridors, the bolshevists could muster only 140 votes out of 423. As usual they refused to submit to the decision of the majority and withdrew from the hall, the loyal members electing Tchernoff as presiding officer. A drunken sailor from the bolshevist ranks was then sent into the chamber and announced: "I am tired of this business. We want to go to bed. We will give you ten minutes more."

The delegates were forced to leave the hall, and when they attempted to assemble again to establish a government for Russia on a sane and stable basis, they found the Bolshevist Government in charge of the Duma hall, holding it down and refusing admittance to any of their members!

By means of force the bolshevists defeated the attempt of the people of Russia to establish for themselves a representative form of government.

On page 945 of the published proceedings of the Senate Investigating Committee, entitled "Bolshevik Propaganda," I find the following question and answer by Senator Knute Nelson and Ambassador Francis:

Senator Nelson: "Has the Bolshevik Government, since that time, ever attempted to have a constituent assembly elected or meet?"

Mr. Francis: "No, sir. They have never since that time had a constituent assembly, or called an election for a constituent assembly."

Backward and downward has ever been their motto, instead of *onward and upward.* The picture presented to the Russian people by Lenin *et al.* was like unto the spectacle one saw at the theatre in my boyhood — all gilt and glitter; beautiful maidens; powerful warriors; shining swords and armour! The reality was but tinsel, painted women, padded tights, imitation tin swords, dressed-up extra men daubed with glistening paint, and dressing rooms reeking with the smell of cigarettes and stale beer!

But Lenin found that "he who overcomes by force hath overcome but half his foe." There is something implanted in the very marrow of humankind that resents dictatorship, and Lenin soon saw that running a government differed from destroying one. It is so easy to find fault — to destroy; so difficult to build up. A man with a stick of dynamite may destroy the work of a century! Monuments are erected to the constructors, the doers; not to the destroyers and fault-finders.

Lenin flew the Red Flag to secure office, but immediately adopted, by his deeds, the Black Flag to maintain himself and his supporters. Irresponsibility begets bitter criticism — responsibility soon teaches the critic the difficulties! Lenin had stood Russia on her head and gone through her pockets! It was now up to him to feed and employ the people, but Russia was under the control of the fault-finders, the critics, the wreckers and wranglers who, all their lives having preached the doctrine of destruction, of course, knew nothing of how to solve the problems of reconstruction. The unarmed people were left helpless and almost starving. The armed were fed, clothed, and given a perpetual holiday. The bourgeoisie were few and had been pampered by special privileges for generations until they were unfit to lead, unready to act, full ripe to submit. The peasantry, scattered over one sixth of the earth's surface, had but little cohesion. Arms there were none; food there was little; leadership was lacking, and ever present was the fear that those who could lead, and would lead, would lead back to czarism.

The people, long accustomed to being ruled by force, submitted in a measure. When they resisted, they were either sent to prison or *murdered.* Under the name of freedom the worst autocracy in the world's history ruled triumphant. Force and violence, assassination and theft became hourly occurrences. All publications which spoke against the present czars were suppressed;

not only the ordinary papers, but socialist papers met the same fate. Free speech came to mean speech that suited Lenin. Equal rights there were none and universal suffrage became a memory.

Russia had been very ill for centuries but the cure of Lenin, the Quack, became worse than the disease. *Russia did not benefit by trading Nicholas II for Nikolai I.* Song and laughter departed from the country. The people found that cloth sometimes looks good in the bolt but wears poorly when made into a suit of clothes. One does not get maple sap out of a mongrel fir; nor could it be expected that men who would accept bribes to betray their own people would change their nature and play square if it was more profitable to be crooked. Where the thought is bad, the act is worse!

Private rights were destroyed. The equal-pay myth lasted but a short time and, step by step, Lenin was forced to retract his valiant promises of the days of agitation. He who was against all armament was forced to maintain a great Red army in order to overawe and control the majority. He said all land should belong to all the people, yet already there is a distribution of ownership based on an attempt to hold the support of the peasantry. He advocated control of factories by the workers, but so small did their product become that to-day, in Russia, the worker is a slave who can neither change nor quit his job. He advocated the creation of a free and voluntary league, but instead created a dictatorship which destroyed all who objected.

But despite the overwhelming evidence printed in the papers and magazines of the world, it is probably necessary to quote in exact language — in their own language — just what the bolshevists of Russia promised; just what they have done and just what they are doing. There may be some question about the guilt of one who pleads "Not guilty," but there can be no question about the guilt of the Russian bolshevists who not only have pleaded "Guilty," but brag of their infamy!

The apologists of bolshevism in our country have striven hard to protect before the bar of public opinion of our people their ruthless friends in Russia. They have, as I said before, made claims for the bolshevists that the bolshevists themselves indignantly deny. The American (?) liar is prone to claim that the majority of the people of Russia were in favour of bolshevism when Kerensky was overthrown. The preceding facts show this to be false. They claim the bolshevists believe and practise democracy. I quote what the socialist, William English Walling, has to say on this point in his work: "Russia's Message," written in 1907 after having talked with Lenin:

I was shocked to find that this important leader also, though he expects a full cooperation with the peasants on equal terms during the revolution, feels toward them a very deep distrust, thinking them to a large extent bigoted and blindly patriotic, and fearing that they may some day shoot down the revolutionary workingmen as the French peasants did during the Paris Commune.

The chief basis for this distrust is, of course, the prejudiced feeling that the peasants are not likely to become good socialists. It is on account of this feeling that Lenin and all the social democratic leaders place their hopes on a future development of modern large agricultural estates in Russia and the increase of the landless agricultural working class, which alone they believe would prove truly socialist. At the same time, Lenin is far more open-minded on the subject than the leaders formerly in control of the party and conceded it was possible that such peasants or farmers as were not at the same time employers might join in a future socialist movement.

We see at the same time that their leading political party expects the city working people to maintain the chief role and that the confidence of the leaders of this party in the peasantry is without any deep roots.

On the same page Mr. Walling says: "Lenin never did believe in democracy, nor does he practise it."

A democracy without universal suffrage? Impossible, you say, of course, but in the very constitution itself, published in the *Nation* and reproduced by the Seattle *Union Record* — that paper with neither a soul nor a country — the following exceptions occur on page 13, Article 4, Chapter 13, under the heading, "The Right to Vote":

65. The following persons enjoy neither the right to vote nor the right to be voted for, namely:

(a) Persons who have an income without doing any work, such as interest from capital, receipts from property, etc.

(b) Private merchants, trade and commercial brokers.

(c) Monks and clergy of all denominations.

(d) Employees and agents of the former, the gendarme corps and the *Okhrana* (Czar's secret service), also members of the former reigning dynasty.

(e) Persons who have in legal form been declared demented or mentally deficient and also persons under guardianship.

(f) Persons who have been deprived, by a soviet, of their rights of citizenship because of selfish or dishonourable offences, for the period fixed by the sentence.

Note particularly article (f): "Persons who have been deprived, by a soviet, of their rights of citizenship because of selfish or dishonourable offences, for the period fixed by the sentence." In other words, we have a soviet, our opponents have a majority; they will overthrow us unless disfranchised. Therefore, we disfranchise them for as long a time as we see fit. There is no appeal. Under this article hundreds and thousands of men who have disagreed have been deprived of their suffrage and right to hold office, *simply because the inverted czarism of Lenin must stifle democracy.* Think of it! Any merchant, or priest, or minister is deprived of his vote, even though he be a member of the army or navy! A soldier or sailor cannot vote or hold office if he receives rent, interest, or profit, or employs a labourer to help him till the soil.

I quote again from an article by Lenin himself, published in April, 1918, in the New International, an American bolshevist publication:

The word democracy cannot be scientifically applied to the *Communist Party.* Since March, 1917, the word democracy is simply a *shackle fastened upon the revolutionary nation* and preventing it from establishing boldly, freely, regardless of all obstacles (*such as the people's will*), a new form of power — the Council of Workmen, Soldiers and Peasants' Deputies, harbinger of the abolition of *every form of authority.*

Also in January, 1917, Lenin said:

Just as 150,000 lordly landowners under czarism dominated the 130,000,000 of Russian peasants, so 200,000 bolsheviki are imposing their proletarian will on the mass, but this time in the interest of the latter.

Nothing can be plainer than that remark unless it be these:

A fairly prosperous working man is not a proletariat.
Only the very poorest peasant or working man can vote.

In speaking of the restriction of suffrage invoked by Lenin and his follow-ers, soon after they seized the power of government, Charles Edward Russell in his book, , "Bolshevism and the United States," says:

After the bolshevists had seized the government offices and proclaimed Lenin as Prime Minister, a change was made in the franchise and the system of election. It had been the boast of intelligent Russians that after the Revolution all citizens of Russia, men or women, stood upon one plane of equality, in an absolute de-mocracy. They were not long allowed such a distinction. The new system adopt-ed after the bolshevik coup provided that delegates to the provincial Soviets (which elected the delegates to the National Soviet) should be chosen on this basis:
For every 125 soldiers, or Red Guards, as they were called after Lenin's tri-umph, one delegate;
For every 1,000 factory workers or others belonging to what was called the working class, one delegate;
For every *volost*, or union of peasants' villages, two delegates.
Perhaps you do not get the whole meaning of this until you know that a *volost* may contain from 10,000 to 100,000 inhabitants, and seldom has fewer than 15,000. Say the average is 20,000, which is a low estimate, the popular franchise in Russia would work out thus:
Every soldier has one vote;
Every factory worker has one eighth of a vote;
Every peasant has one eightieth of a vote.

Our farmers and factory workers would certainly be pleased if we had such an arrangement in the United States! Offer the American farmer one eighti-eth of a vote and you would be lucky to escape with your life.
In speaking of the right of assembly, Russell says:

The *Northern Commune* of September 13th publishes the decree of Zinoviev, one of Lenin's most active and famous assistants, covering this matter.

4. Three days' notice must be given to the soviet, or to the Committee of the Village Poor, of all public and private meetings.

5. All meetings must be open to the representatives of the soviet power — *viz.,* the representatives of the Central and District Soviet, the Committee of the Poor and the Kommandatur of the Revolutionary Secret Police Force.

This was the same as Bismarck's law, passed in order to destroy socialism. So successful was it that in ten years the socialists increased in Germany from 350,000 to 1,600,000.

When Lenin thought he could control the Constituent Assembly *he declared himself in favour of it,* but when he found that his supporters were in a hopeless minority, he dispersed the Assembly. Like the Czar? Yes, but a little worse!

In Article II, Paragraph 23, of the official Constitution, compelled by law to be posted in all public places in Russia, I find:

23. Being guided by the interests of the working class as a whole the Russian Socialist Federated Soviet Republic *deprives all individuals and groups of rights which could be utilized by them to the detriment of the socialist revolution.*

The right of free assembly was abolished by Lenin and the right of free speech came to mean only the right to say those things which would please the ruling power. All men who disagreed with Lenin were called counterrevolutionists and he filled the prisons with such people.

A free press is probably as necessary an element in maintaining the rights of the people as any other one thing, and yet the bolshevists of Russia closed and nailed up the printing plants of even the socialist publications and threw their editors in jail; and this was done despite Paragraph 14 of Chapter V of their own Constitution found on page 1161, U.S. Senate investigation, "Bolshevik Propaganda," which reads:

14. For the purpose of securing for the toilers real freedom of expression of their opinions, the R. S. F. S. R. abolishes the dependence of the press upon capital and places in the hands of the working class and of the poorer elements of the peasantry all the technical and material means for the publication of newspapers, pamphlets, books, and all other press productions and secures their free circulation throughout the country.

Openly repudiating the right of free press, I find Lenin advocating in his "Soviets at Work," as printed by the Seattle *Union Record*:

The merciless suppression of the thoroughly dishonest and insolently slanderous bourgeois press.

Czar Lenin would brook no criticism, whether by the spoken or written word!

Later he says, in speaking of the resistance to soviet rule through publications in the press of the Cadets:

The nearer we get to a complete military suppression of the bourgeoisie, the more dangerous become for us the petty bourgeois anarchic inclinations. They must be combated by *compulsion*.

On the same page he says:

And our rule is too mild, quite frequently resembling jam rather than iron.

And this statement despite his admission of thousands of murders.
Again he complains because.

Our revolutionary and popular tribunals are excessively and incredibly weak,

and this despite the fact that thousands were in prisons while hundreds of thousands more had been intimidated and Lenin-shed blood stained the village greens all over Russia.

Lenin and Trotsky advocated soviet or "group control" of factories, but they soon found that the laws of nature operated even in Russia. They then decided to place the government-owned industries of Russia under an autocratic boss and demanded absolute and complete "labour control." They blame famine and unemployment "on everyone who violates the labour discipline in any enterprise and in any business."

They tried and punished without mercy all men who did not obey without question, boasts Lenin on the next page of the same book.
At this point he says:

The question of principle is, in general, the appointment of individuals endowed with unlimited power, the appointment of dictators.... etc.

On the following page he says:

But how can we secure a strict unity of will? By subjecting the will of thousands to the will of one.

And a little later he adds:

But at any rate, complete submission to a single will is absolutely necessary for the success of the processes of work.... etc.

On the same page I find this:

And to-day the same revolution — and indeed the interest of socialism — demands the absolute submission of the masses to the single will of those who direct the labour process.

One notes that many czarlings of Lenin's creation are to control all workers. The workers of Russia, if they obey Lenin, have nothing to say as to their hours of labour and cannot even quit their jobs. To strike in Russia, of course, would be a crime against the State and the strikers would be shot.

In the United States many of the labour unions have denounced and fought the "Taylor System," which is purported to be the most scientific method of efficient production. In our country, piece work has been denounced as "one of the worst curses Labour has to contend with."

In his "Soviets at Work," I find Lenin advocating this system for Russia when he says:

We should immediately introduce piece work and try it out in practice. We should try out every scientific and progressive suggestion of the Taylor System...etc.

Instead of Bolshevism bringing freedom to the workers, it brought slavery. Instead of independence — submissive dependence! Instead of equal pay for all (the Utopia of the soap-box philosophers) we find that Lenin was forced to engage specialists to try and bring about order in industry, paying them 25,000 to 50,000, yes, even 100,000 rubles per year as he admits in his book.

In spite of the repressive measures adopted by Czar Nikolai, discipline could not be maintained. Production fell off in many instances 75 to 80 per cent, while the people remained hungry, ragged, and even starving. During the winter of 1918 thousands froze to death in a country which has more standing timber than any other in the world. Thousands more starved to death, although Russia has much of the most fertile land of the world.

From my conversations with returning travellers I am convinced that millions would have died of starvation this year if the production of foodstuffs had depended on the demoralized men of Russia. Thousands of them spent their time in idleness, riding free on the railroads from place to place and receiving small rations from the Government.

The women, however, always in every country more conservative and industrious than the men, plowed the ground, sowed the seed, and reaped the harvest, thus saving Russia from the worst famine in its history. When these women get a chance to vote — and that chance will come — *Quack Lenin and Talker Trotsky* will lose their jobs and probably come to the United States, and, under the beneficent protection of our authorities at Washington, become writers for Max Eastman's *Liberator,* or teachers in the "Rand School of Social Science."

Chapter Eleven - The Origin and Development of Bolshevism in the United States

Ideas are cosmopolitan. They have the liberty of the world. — Beecher.
Our land is not more the recipient of the man of all countries than of their ideas. — Bancroft.

WHEN Lenin and Trotsky secured control of Russia they felt that their efforts to metamorphize existing systems must fail unless the movement became international. They knew that their experiment must spread or die of dry rot. They knew that the Red Flag could not wave on the same planet with our flag, the flag of freedom, liberty, and equal rights. Therefore with the help of their employer, Germany, they set out to bring about the overthrow of all other forms of government including our own. Their employer furnished them with unlimited means to destroy other governments. Especially was Germany anxious to bring about chaotic conditions in countries which were at war with her. They proposed to demoralize and devitalize the spirit of national patriotism everywhere, in order, first, to win the war on the battlefield; and second, to win the greater war of trade and expansion afterward.

Lenin and Trotsky were willing workers. They were ready to use the methods of propaganda advocated and paid for by Germany but their purpose primarily was firmly to establish internationally the bolshevist government, and they cared not by what means such an end was attained. Germany supported the bolshevist counter revolution as did the monarchists of Russia, believing that it was an ephemeral thing, would fall in a few days, and then absolutism could again take the saddle. Germany, as usual, was wrong in judging the psychology of men. Lenin and Trotsky, with Germany's help, secured control of Russia but then established, as we have seen, an autocracy supported, as every autocracy must be supported, by an armed force. Germany had forgotten that for centuries the Czar had, by means of his army, maintained tyranny despite the wishes of the people of Russia. Germany apparently never realized that Lenin would follow in the Czar's footsteps, and use the identical methods, only made more stringent, to maintain himself in power.

The moment the bolsheviki disdained popular support, repudiated universal suffrage, and recruited a great army that was well fed and paid, that moment Germany's hope of a temporary bolshevism faded away. Bolshevism in Russia will last just so long as her force in the field is the *strongest force*. Argument is of no avail. The fact that the majority is against Lenin means nothing. The bolsheviki see to it that the army is maintained and the army sees to it that bolshevism is maintained! You scratch my back and I'll scratch yours! Either a larger force must destroy Lenin's army or the army itself must be permeated with dissatisfaction and revolt; otherwise the Government as now conducted in Russia will continue indefinitely; provided always that food and clothing in sufficient quantities are available for the maintenance of the health and strength of the soldiers.

Germany, no doubt, believed that the crushing treaty, forced by her upon Russia, would destroy the bolshevist regime. She, no doubt, expected to win the war and then turn her armed forces against the Red Army. However, the fortunes of war went against the Teutons and their surrender ended any chance of their intervention.

Just as soon as Lenin firmly held the reins of power, he sent his zealots to other countries to spread the doctrines of revolution. No land was immune. Ireland, England, Austria, Hungary, Italy, France, Egypt, India, etc., as well as our own land, received their quota of men and women whose duty it was to destroy, in order to rebuild from the ruins, a government such as Russia had inaugurated.

Thousands came to our shores; thousands more were already here, fully primed for action, only awaiting the transported spark to set ablaze a destructive fire. In a desultory way, bolshevism had existed in the United States for many years. The Noble and Holy Order of the Knights of Labour, organized in 1869, embraced syndicalism in many of its manifestations. By 1887 they had more than one million members. Their main object was to destroy the wage system and craft unionism. Although the leaders preached against sabotage and violence, the members practised both. This was effectually demonstrated in the southwest railway strike in 1886.

In 1883 a convention was held in Pittsburg, composed of direct action groups from all over the United States. They issued a definite proclamation declaring for the destruction of the existing government by revolutionary and international action, and demanded the exchange of goods between producers without profit.

Johann Most, anarchist, was the father of this movement in this country, and once again honest Labour suffered the penalty of the preaching and practice of anarchy. This movement culminated in the Haymarket Massacre in Chicago, in 1886, which affair had a most disastrous effect on the labour movement. The preaching of anarchy for a time passed out of existence, but because of it Labour had received a serious setback.

The doctrines taught were all one with those of Michael Bakounin, beginning by being atheistic and always ending with direct action. One writer of note, Robert Hunter, says:

The Labour movement lay stunned after its brief flirtation with anarchy. Without a doubt, the bomb in Chicago put back the Labour movement for years.

Every time Labour associates with syndicalists, Labour is the sufferer, usually the only one, and yet time and again false, power-mad syndicalists in labour circles start the same old quack cure-all on its rounds, often deceiving thousands.

Now enters Eugene V. Debs, several times since candidate for President on the socialist ticket, and who is now in a Federal penitentiary for violation of the Espionage Act. Eugene V. Debs, in June, 1893, organized the American Railway Union in Chicago. This was an industrial union having many of the characteristics of syndicalism. Within a short time Debs led the Pullman strikers to defeat, after tying up most of the railroads of the country and bringing many cities to the verge of starvation.

Debs, at this time, was a magnetic personality. Tall, angular, of dauntless courage and determination, he stood head and shoulders above his associates. He was a real orator and always meant what he said. As a boy, I had the good fortune to listen to many of the great orators of my time, but Debs always affected me most. He could always make my heart beat faster, and cause my blood to leap and pulse through my veins. His appearance, his sincerity, his simple life, his willingness to sacrifice, the indescribable timbre and vibration of his voice, held me spellbound.

At the time of the Pullman strike Debs was not very well read. He had been a railroad engineer, and his opportunities had been scant, but upon being placed in the Woodstock, Ill., jail, he began to read and study socialism, and he soon became not only a political socialist but a direct-action revolutionist. Until late years, however, red hate did not enter his soul. He was as gentle and kind as Eugene Field and loved humanity and all men. He never had a dollar in his life that you or I could not, for the asking, get half or all of. And one did not have to ask; if he saw you needed the dollar, it was yours. In private life, gentle and kind; on the firing line, he was as brave, resourceful, firm, and unrelenting as Grant.

He never deserted his colours, but, as the years went on, the colours took on a deeper crimson. He lacked poise, balance, and logical sequence of thought, but was not like unto the cowards who lead the Reds of to-day. He took his whiskey straight and never asked the bartender for water. He was wrong, mistaken, had little idea of the true meaning of history, refused to learn from experience, but was brave always. It is too bad that Debs never could understand evolution and hence always believed in revolution.

Debs, through his teachings and agitation, has been very influential in forming the thought of the present-day syndicalists. The Western Federation of Miners carried on an I.W.W. propaganda for years, but it was not until 1905 that the Industrial Workers of the World was organized.

In November, 1904, William Trautmann, editor of the *Brauer Zeitung,* official organ of the United Brewery Workmen; George Estes, president of the United Brotherhood of Railway Employees; W. L. Hall, secretary of the same organization; Isaac Cowen, American representative of the Amalgamated Society of Engineers in Great Britain; Clarence Smith, and Thomas J. Hagerty, a Catholic priest, met in Chicago and with the cooperation and support of Debs, issued a letter calling for a larger meeting in January, 1905. In this letter the fathers of the American I.W.W. said:

We have absolute confidence in the ability of the working class *to take posses-sion of and operate successfully the...the industries of the country.*

In January, the secret conference was held, twenty-three people being present, including Chas. H. Meyer, president of the Western Federation of Miners; A. M. Simons, well-known socialist writer; Frank Bohn, organizer of the Socialist Labour Party, and "Mother" Mary Jones.

This group issued a manifesto demanding equal pay for all work and criticizing the craft union, saying of it: "It generates a system of organized scabbery" and leads "union men to scab on each other." This manifesto declared that the teachings of the American Federation of Labour resulted in ignorance and trade monopolies and fostered the idea of harmony between the employer and employee.

President Gompers of the American Federation of Labour probably said: "Just another crowd of socialists who want to destroy the American trade-union movement." He probably did not foresee the bitter struggle which is now taking place within his own organization, between the I. W.W. element and the progressive, loyal majority.

In June, 1905, two hundred men met in Chicago, and organized the Industrial Workers of the World. Daniel DeLeon, Eugene V. Debs, Haywood Moyer, "Priest" Hagerty, D. C. Coates, and Simons were the dominating factors. Hagerty, the priest, framed the preamble of the I.W.W. Coates later organized the nonpartisan forces in North Dakota.

From that day to this there has been a continual battle between the forces of trade unionism and the supporters of the I.W.W. programme, and this battle will not end until one of the two contending factions destroys the other. It is usually, but not invariably, the case, that those who contend for the most, demand and promise the impossible, and preach "hurry," win over those more moderate and sensible souls who really understand how slow all lasting progress must necessarily be.

So many people seem to be of the opinion that the I.W.W. is simply a radical national labour union. As a matter of fact, the I.W.W. is primarily and fundamentally an international, revolutionary society formed for the purpose of overthrowing *all* present governments, and *all* present systems (except, of course, the I.W.W. Government of Russia), and inaugurating class rule by the dictator who, by taking thought, can change the physical formation of the earth remodel human nature, reconstruct everything, abolish God and good, parachute humanity over all the rough edges of life, and bring about happiness forever after!

But let us quote from the preamble of the Constitution of the I.W.W. itself:

The working class and the employing class have nothing in common. There can be no peace...

You have no difficulty in recognizing the class-hatred teachings of Prince Bakounin in the very first sentence, and the very first sentence is untrue.

As a matter of fact, the men who work have a common interest with the men they work for and *with.* Each has his separate duty to perform in order that industry may progress and function. The employer surely performs a necessary duty by first planning in his mind and then establishing in actuality the factory; the thought almost invariably is his thought; the capital to operate on is his; the first investment is his; the failure of the undertaking causes him loss, oft-times irremediable, while the failure as far as the worker is concerned very, very seldom causes him to lose even a day's pay; for Labour gets its money even though other creditors suffer. Sometimes, however, the failure of a particular industry in a particular place means change of residence as well as unemployment for the worker.

The interests of employer and employee are identical in several ways: first, a successful enterprise, say in Puyallup, Washington, means steady employment for the workers, means the establishment of homes and local ties, means steady schooling for the children, means social life and happiness for all. Success means food, clothing, education, and stability of employment and mode of life; the ability on the part of the worker to plan ahead; to vision, in a measure, his family's future; to feel safe in buying an acre of land, building a home, and paying for it gradually.

Success in this Puyallup undertaking means, for the employer, profitable use of his capital, stability for his investment. A successful enterprise is the only one that can *grant to the worker continuous employment at a decent and living wage.* The ability to furnish continuous and profitable employment to the worker gathers around the factory steady, thrifty men whose output grows in productiveness and value because of their experience and settled condition. This enables the enterprise to pay more to the employer and more to the worker than if it be unprofitable and temporary. If the American owner does his share of the work, if sufficient capital is invested, if Labour does its work, if employer, employee, and administrative heads all do their work, American-made goods can compete with the foreign-made product, and steady employment is the result; but if the enterprise fail in any one of these particulars, it *must close down.* The employer, if he has any capital left, seeks new fields; the worker must find a new place, must probably move, while the far-away competitor produces the goods and is the only gainer.

It is not true that dissension between employer and employees brings good. It brings evil. It is bad. The better they work together, the more goods are produced and the more surplus there is left to divide between the creative members of the enterprise. And let me say right here that the man in overalls is not the only worker. The man with the white collar and unsoiled hands very often works harder than the man who labours only with his hands. My experience has proven to me that men taken as a whole *earn what they get regardless of their position in life!* Certainly there are exceptions, many of them, but the rule holds good.

It is also true that men usually find the niche they are best fitted for in the walks of life. Despite contrary statements, I have found that there usually is a manifest reason for the one's success and the other's failure, and that reason is oft-times the fact that some men will *do without for a time* in order to have more at the end, while others want *theirs every day* in rest, in amusement, in idleness, in clothes, etc. I have no fault to find with either crowd, but I deny the right of the man who spends his dollar to come around after a time and demand half of my saved dollar. That gives him $1.50 out of the $2.00 and it does not seem to me to be fair. One cannot eat one's ice cream and have it, too! Further on the I.W.W. preamble says:

Instead of the conservative motto of "A fair day's wages for a fair day's work," we must inscribe on our banner the *Revolutionary watchword:* "Abolition of the wage system!"

Now we have the crux of their doctrine. They are not interested in securing *their share of what is produced.* They want it all. In the very next sentence they say:

It is the historic mission of the working class to do away with capitalism.

All right! We agree that capitalism has its faults; grave faults and many of them. We agree that the problem of scientifically dividing the product of labour, capital, energy, and brains, as applied to natural resources, has not been fair and equitable. We agree that the millennium has not been reached. We agree that human nature operates on *both sides,* and each side strives to secure more than its appropriate and just share and frequently does secure it. The *Red* employer and *Red* employee have one thing in common: they are both fundamentally thieves. But *with what system shall we supplant capitalism?* Has a better system been discovered? Has any other plan, taken "by and large" as Sam Blythe says, ever functioned with one tenth the success of capitalism? If so, show me!

It is indeed unfortunate for the revolutionists that daily papers and magazines have told the story of Russia and syndicalism. It is unfortunate that history persists in telling the truth in relation to the Utopian schemes of past centuries and their progress-destroying failures. Otherwise, we might wonder what the result would be; *now we know what it must be.* We are not in the dark. The child who falls against the hot stove feels the burn and remembers; the great majority of the people will take the child's word that the stove was hot, and that when he fell against it he was injured. The fellow standing in the doorway may talk his lungs out and argue that falling against the stove would not bum if the child fell on his other side, or if he fell with courage, or if he did not jump away so quickly, but the *child's burns, as you apply the sweet oil, always convince everyone but the weak minded or the fanatic.* The man in the doorway says after every failure: "If we all fall on the stove at the same time, it will not burn." He forgets that heat is a condition of temperature, not of opinion.

The world in its final analysis is ruled by *old experience.* Capitalism thus far has been found to be the best and most scientific method yet devised or tried

110

for human happiness. Turning the clock back to communism, or anarchy, has the same chance of permanent success as we would have in running an ox cart in competition with a motor car. *Progress consists in going forward and not backward!*

Before we proceed further we must clearly understand the three cardinal principles of the I.W.W.

First, they demand the destruction of the American Federation of Labour and all kindred organizations. They call the trade unionist a traitor to the cause of revolution. Labour-union leaders they call *"cadets," "labour parasites," "labour fakirs," "the agents of capitalism," "aristocrats of labour,"* and accuse them in their constitution of misleading Labour and supporting the employer.

Second, they plan and demand the overthrow of all orderly government, and denounce unsparingly all political action or legal means of changing the prevailing laws. They want overthrow of law and order by force and at once. *Now* is always the accepted time!

Third, they demand, after the overthrow, that a few untrained agitators be placed in positions of dictators, *and that everyone who does not agree be either exterminated or forced to join their ranks!*

As to the necessity of continuing production, they speak only in general terms, much as a boy of six does when asked; "What will you do when you grow up?" They apparently have just as definite and certain plans as to what should be done after *Der Tag* as the boy has regarding his future. The answer you get from the boy is certainly more definite and more likely to come to pass than the answer one receives on reading their literature or talking with their evangelists.

In the beginning, the American Federation of Labour ridiculed the I.W.W.'s as a crowd of disappointed office seekers, the *Federationist* calling them "the most stupendous impossibles the world has yet seen."

All the officers elected at their constitutional convention were socialists, but the Socialist Party did not indorse their programme. Haywood carried the fight to the American Federation of Labour, saying: "The ideas of Mr. Gompers are hoary, aged, moss-covered relics of the days of the ox team and pony express."

The battle was on between the craft-union idea and the *one big union*. That battle has been carried on up to the present day, but the I.W.W.'s have usually failed to get and hold the skilled worker, nor have they been able to convince the thinkers in the ranks. One of the great troubles faced by the I.W.W. organization everywhere is the fact that the demoralization of its own members makes them untrustworthy and dishonest. I.W.W. organizers and petty treasurers continually abscond with the funds. Brissenden, in "The I.W.W.: A Study of American Syndicalism," says:

The dearth of ability and especially want of honesty in its managing personnel were to become all too evident...as was also its practically bankrupt condition.

In the words of Haywood, "Industrial unionists should abrogate all agreements." Contracts, morality, and right are as nothing to them. The organization has reaped the fruit of its own teachings. *You cannot tell a man to steal for you and expect him never to steal from you. There is no honour among thieves and never has been!*

Their second convention was held in 1906. The dishonest teachings were already bearing fruit. The auditing committee found that "President Sherman's report shows extravagance and strong evidence of corruption." Speakers at the convention charged "corruption, graft, and fakirization which would put to shame the worst of the American Federation of Labour." Brissenden says in his book just quoted:

> The preaching of the overthrow of all government *took,* and the *Reds* abolished the office of President, and according to President Sherman, "violated the constitution."

Unable even to rule themselves in a small convention of ninety-three of the leaders it would seem quite proper to remark that they probably would fail if given control of the earth and the riches thereof.

It was not long before the I.W.W. split into two bodies, one known as the Detroit I.W.W. and the other as the Chicago I.W.W. The Detroit I.W.W. preaches political action; the Chicago I.W.W., with whose affairs we will deal exclusively, disdains any political action whatever, deeming "force, direct action, sabotage, strike, and revolution, as the only proper means of procedure." The Detroit branch changed their name "in order," said they, "to escape from the smell of the 'bummery' of the Chicago name." They call themselves the W. I. I. U., the Workers' International Industrial Union.

As already stated, those who promise the greatest and most immediate results usually win the greatest number of supporters and converts. This happened with the two factions; the Chicago I.W.W. gaining the most members and exerting the most power. We are not particularly concerned with the civil war between the two bodies. A man whose house is about to be robbed cares little about the quarrel between the burglars. He gains time, however, to call the police while they argue whether it is best to dynamite the basement door or use a jimmy on the bedroom window in the second story.

For many years the I.W.W. had a wandering, unorganized existence, being always strongest in the Far West and weakest in the states where industry was highly developed and home life more stable.

The so-called free-speech fights carried on at intervals were not fights for free speech and were not intended to be. They were simply petty quarrels picked by the organization for the purpose of bill-boarding their supposed importance. In Los Angeles in 1911, however, when the *Times* Building was blown up by dynamite and several people killed, the organization really practised its theories.

All my readers will recall the great effort made to gain organized Labour's support for the McNamaras; parades were held, funds were collected, the innocence of the murderers was emblazoned on banners, and a general strike was to be called to terrify the law-enforcing officials, and then the McNamaras confessed to the crime, and Labour once more, after "flirting with anarchists," received a black eye, and was made to appear ridiculous.

Some day honest Labour will learn that it is forced to carry the water and cut the wood for these anarchists, and is always blamed if failure comes, but never gets the credit if success is attained. The I.W.W. cry loudly for help when in trouble, and just as soon as Labour has helped them out, they "bite the hand that fed them."

The McNamaras' crime was but one of a long series carried out by them and their fellows; they operated everywhere and dealt openly in murder and theft. I was greatly complimented when McNamara, in prison, gave out an interview attacking my acts during the general strike. It is fine to know that such men are against you. It makes you feel good and convinces honest men you were 100 per cent, right.

From 1911 on the I.W.W. became more and more openly hostile to government. In all their publications they demanded direct action, until to-day direct action with its sabotage, strike, and destructive tactics generally, constitutes *all their methods*.

In 1912 they took entire charge of the Lawrence, Mass., textile strike. Joseph Ettor and Wm. D. Haywood led this strike, which developed every phase of revolutionary syndicalism. For instance, the *Survey* quotes a Lawrence resident as describing as follows the way the I.W.W. operated:

The addresses of the men working are given to a committee. They are visited after nine o'clock at night by strangers, generally Poles.
"Working to-day?" (The man speaking has a sharp knife and is whittling a stick.)
"Yah."
"Work to-morrow?"
"Id' no."
"If you work to-morrow, I cut your throat."
"No, no, I no work."
"Shake," and they shake hands.
Wm. D. Haywood tried to bring about a general strike in Lawrence, saying: "We will tie up the railroads, put the city in darkness and starve the soldiers out."

When Ettor and Giovannitti, I.W.W. orators, were placed in jail, the Seventh National Convention of the organization was being held. They *demanded immediate release and acquittal of these two men no matter what the facts were and threatened that the industries of the country would suffer a general strike unless their demands were obeyed.* In other words, in open convention the I.W. W., in the year of our Lord 1912, openly advocated and threatened the general strike unless the judge and jury who were to try accused individuals, who happened to be members of their order, let the accused go free.

The I.W.W. propaganda sheets openly demanded sabotage. "They demanded a boycott on Lawrence, asked railroad men to lose their cars, telegraphers to lose their messages, etc," said Brissenden in his book already quoted.

The merits or demerits of the strike is not the question. The outstanding accomplishment of the strike was that a body of syndicalists in America were allowed to preach and practise violence and sabotage and "*get away with it.*"

A banner carried in a strikers' parade read:

> ARISE!!! SLAVES OF THE WORLD!!!!
>
> NO GOD!! NO MASTER!!!

The tenets and practices of the syndicalists of long ago were adopted from cocktails to small blacks. The leaders gained in courage and vituperative violence. They had dared the Government and won. They had broken the plain law and escaped. They had both preached and practised and were not punished. *They now spread all over the United States.*

In September, 1914, they held another convention. They said: "Don't parade and ask help from politicians. Go where there is plenty of food and clothing and help yourselves."

As reported in the Chicago *Daily News* of Sept. 22, 1914, Haywood said:

Take what you need where you find it. It is yours. Take food, clothing, shelter. Take over machinery. Use it for yourselves. It is yours.

Frank Little, who was afterward hanged in Butte, said: "Wherever I go I inaugurate sabotage among the workers."

The convention went on record "as refusing to fight for any purpose except industrial freedom."

The great war in Europe was in its initial stages. The fight between the American Federation of Labour and the I.W.W. grew more bitter daily. The Federationists charged that the I.W.W.'s "scabbed on the job" in order to destroy the Federation. The I.W.W. would inaugurate a strike. The A. F. of L. would have agreements between the employers and the engineers who were not on strike, and yet the industry could not be tied up without the engineers repudiating their agreement with the employers. Many times the A. F. of L. men would stay on the job. Then the I.W.W. called *them* scabs. Many I. W. W's had, against the rules of their order, joined the A. F. of L. unions in order to secure work, but night and day they tried to disunionize their associates.

Many I.W.W.'s and their sympathizers openly denounced the war in Europe and just as openly, later on, denounced our entrance into the war, when our Government became convinced of the necessity of such action. Following in their wake were the pacifists and all that mongrel breed who would partake of all the good that comes from our form of government, while refusing to defend it. They were everywhere. The draft law or conscription act was their especial target. Caring neither for the future of the world nor for giving a fair chance to our own boys in the trenches, they made every effort to

114

check our war preparations, cause the failure of the Liberty Loans, etc. The I.W.W. element, *left unchecked and unpunished in time of peace, came back to plague our nation in time of war.*

Many of the I.W.W.'s were arrested during the war and some were punished. The Government started, stopped, started again, conciliated, pandered, and generally pursued a skim-milk policy. Argument was tried, kindness, public statements appealing to patriotism, and this to a class of men who know but one argument, *force;* who think kindness is weakness, and who have no patriotism!

It might be well in order that the reader may understand the activities of the I.W.W. to go more fully into the spoken and written tenets, beliefs, methods, and practices of this organization. So many people look upon the violence as sporadic, incidental, individual, instead of the work of the organization itself.

Any honest man who investigates the I.W.W. must come to the following conclusions:

First, the I.W.W. is an international revolutionary society and not a labour union.

Second, it is against all labour unions, against all government, and aims at the overthrow of all organized society.

Third, it teaches class hatred, direct action, use of force and violence, sabotage on the job; brings on strike after strike for *no other reason than to cause the workers to hate the employers and the Government.*

Fourth, it believes and teaches that after strike after strike has been called, the worker will grow to hate the employer *and will hate the Government whose function it is to preserve order.* This prepares the worker for revolution.

Fifth, it believes revolution must be brought about by means of the general strike which shall paralyze industry and deprive the people of the necessities of life.

Sixth, it is against any preparedness programme which would give the Government an armed force to protect itself when *Der Tag* comes.

Seventh, it is against all religion and all morality. The I.W.W. has found it necessary to destroy all established modes of thought and conduct in order to prepare the worker's mind for violence, theft, arson, murder, the *Red Terror*, and free love.

Eighth, the I.W.W. members not only believe In the above programme, not only teach it, but each and everyone puts into practice these beliefs as far as his opportunities and courage permit him so to do!

Ninth, all cooperation and peace are abhorrent to the I.W.W. as well as all orderly legal means of action. *Force is the only method they will consider.*

Tenth, the I.W.W. believes the majority is unfit to control its affairs, but that a minority composed of I.W.W. members should rule and control all things and all men.

I hereby submit proofs which I believe sufficient to convince any reasonable man of the truth of these assertions.

In every town and city during my trip for the Victory Loan through the East I found this organization preaching its doctrines, fomenting class strife, and denouncing all governments alike. In conversation with some of the leading men of the nation I found an appalling ignorance as to this organization — *The Industrial Workers of the World* — its aims, its methods, and its doctrines. Many seemed to believe it was simply a radical labour union with no fundamental beliefs except to make conditions better for the men who toil. It is time the people of this country, my country, learn the truth.

I have been unable to find a more terrific indictment of I.W.W.'ism than its own authoritative records; its own principles enunciated in its own Constitution. Every statement I have made is substantiated by the organization's own printed matter. I have made no effort to convict the organization of anything to which it has not pleaded guilty. This is simply a gathering together and restatement of what it has, times without number, admitted itself.

One of the strangest phenomena observable at all times is the inclination of large numbers of people to believe that some new panacea has been discovered to solve the ills to which humanity is heir. Time and again I have talked with I.W.W. propagandists and they seldom knew that their doctrines had been agitated, and in several instances given a complete trial, nearly a century ago. They all apparently believe that their teachings come from the *"proletariat"*; that they are the discovery of the *Workers of the World* and would, if applied, emancipate all.

The faith of the followers of I.W.W.'ism is only exceeded by the colossal conceit of its leaders. I.W.W.'ism, *bolshevism,* and *revolutionary syndicalism* are one and the same thing. Long before *Lenin* or *Trotsky* or *Haywood* were born, the creed was fully developed and had failed in practice.

The plans of *syndicalism* or I.W.W.'ism, briefly stated, are as follows: to secure the support of a militant minority; refuse universal suffrage to the people; preach continuous and never-ending class war; disfranchise everyone but the poorest shop workers; allow only the *"proletariat"* to vote; cast out even their votes unless they stand four-square with *syndicalism;* join existing labour organizations; gain control of these bodies; bring on strike after strike for the purpose of fomenting discontent and encouraging resentment among the workers against their employers. After each strike is lost, sabotage is to be used on every possible occasion, and when the time is ripe, this militant minority is to *strike down the existing government through the means of a general strike;* take possession of the reins of government, allowing only those who agree with them a voice in the control of affairs; force all other classes to starve or join the *"proletariat";* confiscate all property; wipe out of existence by blood all opposition, and then sail away on a *rainbow of dreams to a blessed land!*

I repeat the I.W.W. is not a labour organization, is not an American organization, but is an *international revolutionary society* whose aim is the over-

116

throw of *all governments,* and the inauguration of a minority rule. or the dictatorship of the *"proletariat."* In every printed article since its inception every leader has openly denounced and despised the majority. They say in all their documents that the majority do not know what is good for them but that *"we, the self-chosen leaders of the minority,* do know, and the only way to bring about universal happiness is to place us in charge of all things."

This programme was the exact procedure which took place in Russia when the Kerensky Government was overthrown. In the preamble the bolshevists (the Russian I.W.W.'s) naively state:

In order to cure all the ills of humanity, we adopt this constitution...etc.

The I.W.W. teach word for word, and sentence for sentence, the same doctrines as the French syndicalists and the bolshevists. The methods of the I.W.W. and its teachings are exactly the same: class war; strike after strike; *sabotage;* finally the *Great Day;* and then *Happiness forever.* The I.W.W. Constitution says:

There is but one bargain that the I.W.W. will make with the employing class — complete control of industry to the *organized workers* [the I.W.W.'s].

And again:

As a revolutionary organization the I.W.W. aims to use any and all tactics that will get the results sought...The tactics used are determined solely by the power of the organization to make good in their use.

They also say:

No terms are final with the employer; all peace is but an armed truce...No part of the organization is allowed to enter into time contracts with the employers...The I.W.W. seek no agreements with their employers; they claim no concession except that which we have the power *to take and to hold* by the strength of our organization. Failing to force concessions from the employers by the strike, work is resumed and sabotage is used to force the employers to concede to the demands of the workers.

If the employers do not accede to their demands, they go back on the job, practise sabotage; in other words, *strike on the job* by burning buildings, putting spikes in logs, emery dust in machinery, missending trains, spoiling food, causing industrial accidents, and hampering in every manner, by secrecy and stealth, the successful conduct of enterprise. The I.W.W. teachings, without any equivocations or attempted excuses, state plainly that anything that is done which harms industry or government is right.

The teaching and advocacy of sabotage, force, violence, theft, and arson, has blunted and oft-times destroyed the moral sense of the organization's members. They teach non-observance of all law, ridicule morality, advocate godlessness, and are made to believe that everything done by them is *right.*

They also are taught to commit all crimes by *secrecy and stealth, but cautioned to take care of and protect their worthless lives.*

For fear that many readers may think that only a few members believe and practise law-breaking as a duty, I will quote from some of their own literature and from their writers, speakers, and leaders, to prove that every I.W.W. is a *revolutionist, per se,* who is taught to commit crime as a duty, to hate all government, to destroy all orderly society, and *does commit just the number of crimes that his courage, opportunity, and ability permit.*

Wm. D. Haywood — who, thank God, was convicted by that most sensible and loyal jury in the city of Chicago, in the second of his pamphlets, called "The General Strike," published by the I.W.W. Publishing Bureau of Chicago says:

Forty years ago to-day there began the greatest general strike known in modern history, the French Commune.

Later he adds:

There are three phases of a general strike. They are: A general strike in an industry; A general strike in a community; A general national strike.

And again he says:

The American Federation of Labour couldn't have a general strike if they wanted to. They are not organized for a general strike. They have 27,000 different agreements that expire 27,000 different minutes of the year. They will either have to break all those sacred contracts or there is no such thing as a general strike in that so-called "Labour organization." I said *"so-called"*; I say so advisedly. It is not a Labour organization; it is simply a combination of job trusts.

He continues:

If the workers can organize so that they can stand idle they will then be strong enough so that they can take the factories. Then we lock the bosses out and run the factories to suit ourselves. That is our programme. We will do it. You must not be content to come to the ballot box on the first Tuesday after the first Monday in November — the ballot box erected by the capitalist class, guarded by capitalist henchmen — and deposit your ballot to be counted by *black-handed thugs,* and say; "That is political action." I believe that the American Federation of Labour won't take in the working class. They don't want the working class. It isn't a working-class organization. A strike is an incipient revolution. Many large revolutions have grown out of a small strike. If I didn't think that the general strike was leading on to the great revolution, I wouldn't be here.

Later, in speaking of Mexico, he says:

Incidentally, the revolutionists, Magon, Villareal, Sarabia, and Rivera, and their followers, have something to do with it, and also the local unions of the Industrial Workers of the World, there now being at this time three locals whose entire membership have gone across the line and joined the insurgents, and Berthold, one of the commandants, is an officer in the I.W.W. at Holtville, Cal.

A. E. Woodruff, in "Evolution of Industrial Democracy," says:

The Industrial Workers of the World not only martials the workers properly upon the economic field but drills and disciplines them for the *final test of their strength and solidarity, the social general strike,* which is regarded as the culmination of the class struggle.

Not only is the I.W.W. against the Government, and its fundamental principles revolutionary, but it is also the bitter foe of all organized labour. The I.W.W. holds that all labour organizations which do not subscribe to and follow the principles enumerated by them are capitalist unions even though their members are workers.
Vincent St. John, in "The I.W.W.," says:

The craft form of union, with its principle of trade autonomy and harmony of interest with the boss, has also proven a failure. They have become allies of the employers to keep in subjection the vast majority of the workers. The I.W.W. denies that the craft-union movement is a labour movement. We deny that it can or will become a labour movement. In short, the I.W.W. advocates the use of militant "direct-action" tactics to the, full extent of our power to *make good.* The future belongs to the I.W.W. The day of the skilled worker is past.

In speaking of the American Federation of Labour, Vincent St. John says:

This worn-out and corrupt system offers no promise of improvement and adaptation. Union men scab upon union men.

T. Glynn, of the I.W.W. Publishing Co., in "Industrial Efficiency and Its Antidote," tells how efficient the industrial system has become and then carefully explains how to make it less efficient. He also attacks trades unionism as the workers' main foe, and ends his article by stating:

The vacillating and compromising policy of Trade Unionism will no longer suffice. A virile organization, *knowing no law but that of expediency, ready at all times to advance the interests of the working class, is an absolute necessity.*

Chapter Twelve - The Gradual Penetration of the American Federation of Labour by the Industrial Workers of the World

UNTIL a short time ago there was a continuous battle going on between the I.W.W.'s and the A. F. of L. unions of the West. The I.W.W.'s refused to become members of the unions affiliated with the American Federation of La-bour. In time of strike they "scabbed" on the Federation workers, but after we entered the war they changed their tactics and are now "boring from within" and are becoming members of the American Federation of Labour unions all over the United States, and using their assemblies and conventions as a means of spreading their propaganda. They hate Samuel Gompers and men of his kind a great deal worse than they hate any other class of men. They call them labour fakirs, labour parasites, representatives of the capital-ist class, and claim that they are misleading the workers of the nation.

In Seattle, the Red or the I.W.W. faction has secured control of many labour unions. The average worker has a home, a wife, a garden. He pays his dues to his union, but spends his spare time the same as you and I do — at home, at the theatre, at church, in the garden, and with his family. The I.W.W. member seldom has a family, more seldom a home! Still more seldom is he a member of any religious body, as the organization is anti-Christ; he usually lives in lodging houses, seldom has a vote (75 per cent, at least being unnaturalized), so he has plenty of time to attend meetings, and through agitation, organiza-tion, and playing politics, very often is able to elect brother I.W.W.'s to the different union offices. From that time on all dissenters are howled down, refused the right to free speech, insulted and threatened, until the decent body of peace-loving workers allow the militant revolutionary minority to control their affairs. This has happened so often in recent labour history that it was with great pleasure that I read of the Annual Convention of the Ameri-can Federation of Labour held at Atlantic City, disowning and ridiculing the I.W.W. propositions and resolutions which were offered from the floor.

We read in all works of the Industrial Workers of the World, even in their official song books, of *sabotage*. Mr. Webster, in his dictionary, fails to define it, but we learn from Webster that a *sabot* is a wooden shoe used by the French peasants. The wooden shoe is used as the symbol or emblem of the Industrial Workers everywhere. All I.W.W.'s preach *sabotage*. Every I.W.W. that can do so *practises sabotage!* It is a universal and fundamental part of their creed. No I.W.W., *except when on trial,* has ever denied that he believed in and practised *sabotage*.

I hereby submit several quotations from a book entitled "Sabotage," by Elizabeth Gurley Flynn, one of the most noted I.W.W. agitators, published by the I.W.W. Publishing Bureau at 112 Hamilton Ave., Cleveland, Ohio. In the opening paragraph of her book she says:

I am not going to attempt to justify sabotage on any moral ground. If the work-ers consider that sabotage is necessary, *that in itself makes sabotage moral.*

Mrs. Flynn later says:

Sabotage is to this class struggle what the guerrilla warfare is to the battle. The strike is the open battle of the class struggle, sabotage is the guerrilla warfare, the day-by-day warfare between two opposing classes. Sabotage means primarily: *The withdrawal of efficiency.* Sabotage means either to slacken up and interfere with the quantity, or to botch in your skill and interfere with the quality of capitalist production or to give poor service.

In describing how sabotage works in the dyeing of silks, she says:

So whenever they were supposed to be mixing green we saw to it that they put in red, and when they were supposed to be mixing blue we saw to it that they put in green.

And she further explains:

We will let the kegs of wine go over the docks. We will have great boxes of fragile articles drop in the midst of the pier.

She gives still another illustration, as follows:

Suppose he went into a restaurant and ordered a lobster salad, and he said to the spick-and-span waiter standing behind the chair, "Is the lobster salad good?" "Oh, yes, sir," said the waiter, "it is the very best in the city." That would be acting the good wage slave and looking out for the employer's interest. But if the waiter should say, "No, sir, it's rotten lobster salad. It's made from the pieces that have been gathered together here for the last six weeks," that would be the waiter who believed in sabotage, that would be the waiter who had no interest in his boss's profits, the waiter who didn't give a continental whether the boss sold lobster salad or not.

No comment is necessary. These are the basic principles and ideals upon which this organization is founded. They start out with the proposition that whatever they do is *right* and that the *moral law is abrogated*; that the employee is justified in saying anything or doing anything as long as it injures society.

Mrs. Flynn thus closes her comments on sabotage:

I have not given you a rigidly defined thesis on sabotage because sabotage is in the process of making. Sabotage itself is not clearly defined. Sabotage is as broad and changing as industry, as flexible as the imagination and passions of humanity. Every day working men and women are discovering new forms of sabotage, and the stronger their rebellious imagination is, the more sabotage they are going to invent, the more sabotage they are going to develop.

Elizabeth Gurley Flynn is but one of the many I.W.W. writers who justify criminality on the part of the I.W.W. members.

John Graham Brooks is one of the latest authorities on sabotage. In a chapter entitled "Sabotage" in one of his books he says:

From the wooden shoe of the peasant, *sabot,* it has acquired all its mischievous significance. A French syndicalist says it became popular after striking weavers, in 1834, in Lyons, had smashed both glass and machines with their heavy footgear.

Arthur D. Lewis in his book, "Syndicalism and the General Strike," says:

There are other useful forms of "direct-action" sabotage, or the destruction of property, intimidation of the masters, sitting in factories with folded arms, etc.

John Spargo (socialist), in speaking of sabotage, says:

It is all the more remarkable because the syndicalists themselves have recognized the primitive nature of the weapon. To the socialists, sabotage is a form of class warfare to be shunned, principally because it destroys the morale of the working class and unfits it for the proletarian struggle.

Later, Spargo tells us:

Cutting telegraph wires, driving spikes in logs in the lumber-camps in the hope that they will later destroy the saws in the mills, putting cement in the railway switches and dropping monkey wrenches into machinery, are unfortunately common incidents in the industrial struggle.

In commenting further on sabotage he says:

Sabotage is not an efficient weapon of class warfare. It destroys the moral fibre of the man who practises it...Everywhere the organized socialist movement combats the syndicalist advocacy of sabotage as a weapon of class warfare.

Walker C. Smith, who has enjoyed the hospitality of our Seattle jail several times, and is a well-known I.W.W., says, in the foreword of a pamphlet called "Sabotage":

The object of this work is to awaken the producers to a consciousness of their industrial power. It is dedicated not to those who advocate but to those *who use sabotage.*

He says also:

Sabotage may mean the damaging of raw materials, spoiling of a finished product, displacements of parts of machinery, working slow, giving overweight to customers, poor work, missending packages, telling of trade secrets, etc. Due to effective, widespread, systematic sabotage, the brick masons in England lay, as a day's work, less than one third the number of bricks required from their brother craftsmen in America. Sabotage is a direct application of the idea that property has no rights *that its creators are bound to respect.* The question is not: Is sabotage immoral? but: Does sabotage get the goods? The militia can be made useless by the extension of the use of sabotage. When a trainload of soldiers is dispatched the train can be sabotaged. A bar of soap in the boiler would keep the soldiers at home. Sabotage will put a stop to war. If workers are imported, cannot *saboteurs* get on the job in the guise of scabs? Armed with the knowledge of sabotage the workers return to their tasks more terrible in defeat than in victory. Sabotage may mean the *direct destruction of property.*
Should the victory of the workers be forestalled by state socialism, or governmental ownership, it would be a signal for an increased use of sabotage on the part of

the industrialists. The postal employees need run no risk of being court-martialed or even dismissed from the service. In mass sabotage they have a weapon which may be used in an entirely legal but none the less effective manner. Will you arise in your outraged manhood and take a stand for sabotage?

Creatures like Walker C. Smith publish such doctrines, teach them upon every occasion, brag of their defiance of law and order, and *the United States Government apparently can find no law to send them where they belong, to the Federal penitentiaries.*

It may be of interest to the reader to know that putting spikes in logs, thus endangering fellow workers' lives, destroying machinery, turning logging engines loose to run wild down the mountain sides, putting rodents in food, burning down mills, etc., have been in general practice in the lumber woods of the Pacific Coast. When the war broke out it was found necessary to organize the Loyal Legion of Loggers and Lumbermen *in order to produce the spruce for airplanes necessary to win the war.* The I.W.W. used every imaginable device to stop production necessary to give our boys an equal chance on the battle fronts of Europe. They fought against our war programme every day and every minute.

There has never been a single pamphlet issued, a speech made, or propaganda campaign conducted by the I.W.W. where sabotage was not advocated! There is not a factory or logging camp in the world that employs I.W.W.'s where sabotage is not practised. All through their pamphlets and song books tales are told of sabotage being committed, and suggestions are made as to new methods of destruction.

This continuous and never-ending propaganda has brought forth fruit and I could, if desired, fill every page of this book with authentic records of sabotage practised in the lumber camps of Washington and Oregon alone. Beginning in the fall of 1916 and continuing to the present day there has been a persistent effort to destroy this great industry and make its continuance unprofitable. No camp has been immune from the syndicalist.

The *Industrial Worker* of Seattle was the propaganda medium for a long time. In its issue of October 20, 1916, it published a notice requesting the workers to organize to control industry. At the end of the notice these words appeared:

Send in your name and $2.00. Secrecy will be observed. We use plain envelopes to fool the boss.

In Idaho, Montana, Oregon, and Washington agitation for strike after strike has never ceased. After a series of strikes has tested the "worker's mettle" and made him "hate the boss," sabotage on the job is always practised extensively. At the plant of the North Bend Lumber Company, North Bend, Ore., in May, 1918, three large saws were broken in a few days by spikes which had been driven into the logs. These were always driven through the bark so they could not be detected by inspection. This not only delayed work after the breaking of the saws, but was very dangerous to human life. The *Industrial Worker* of May 26th comments as follows on the North Bend sabotage:

The *first* one [spike] did not occasion much talk, but the subsequent two did.

The Industrial Worker of July 28, 1917, states:

A general strike was openly advocated at Dreamland Rink, in Seattle, in July, 1917. Kate Sadler, Red Doran, T. F. H. Dougherty, and other I.W.W.'s spoke for the strike.

Sam Sadler was afterward convicted of sedition as already mentioned and Red Doran was one of the I.W.W.'s convicted at the Chicago trial.

On July 24th there were only two small camps working near Aberdeen, Wash. Camps in Oregon and Washington were completely closed by the I.W.W. agitation in August. The great majority of the camps in other states were either running on part time or were closed down. There was a great reduction in output and this hindered the Government in getting spruce for airplanes. Just before the general lumber strike, which occurred in 1917, after war was declared, an I.W.W. leader was arrested at Spokane. Although his arrest put a damper on the strike, sabotage was ordered on every job.

As said the *Industrial Worker* of July 14, 1917:

Sabotage at Aberdeen took the form of slowing up at Schaefer's Camp; a full crew cut only nineteen logs in a day. They were ordered to speed up by the boss, but all quit and went to town. The same thing occurred at Saginaw Camp No. 5.

At Hoquiam, Wash., a paper commented on March 17th that "many saws had been broken by spikes driven in the logs."

Said the *Seattle Times,* July 14, 1917:

By the middle of June thirteen camps had been shut down near Hoquiam.

George F. Russell, former postmaster of Seattle, said:

I found a solid piece of railroad steel, nearly a foot long, in a log. The bark had been taken off and the rail had been put in and the bark nailed on again.

The *Seattle Times* of July 15, 1917, said:

On July 14th fire broke out in the Lester Logging Camp east of Montesanom, Wash., and spread to other camps. This was caused by the I.W.W.

The same paper reported:

On July 18th timber fire was started in the West Fork Lumber Company's holdings. This was attributed to the I.W.W.

And again:

On July 21st W. M. Emery, chairman of the State Forestry Board, wired Fred E. Pape, State Fire Warden, that "he believed the I.W.W.'s were setting fires to the timber of the Black Diamond Logging Company."

The *Post Intelligencer* of July 25, 1917, said:

On July 24th three I.W.W.'s, Tom Nolan, E. A. Matson, and Robert Solem, the latter an alien, were arrested by the forest rangers for interfering with the fire fighters who were fighting forest fires near Port Angeles, Wash.

The *Seattle Times* of August 16, 1917, reported:

On August 16th fire destroyed 200,000 feet of lumber in the plant of W. J. Lunn at Auburn, Wash., credited to I.W.W.

R. E. Forbes, of the Forbes Timber Company, gave out the following interview September 10, 1919. He said:

The most effective manner of sabotage has been by restricting the output. This is the main cause for the high prices of lumber. For instance, one high lead side has a capacity of yarding and loading ten cars per eight-hour day. Thirty-five men are needed as a working force. It happened that the head logger in our camp was the chief wobbley [I.W.W.]. He was boss of the gang. The hook tender, who is in charge of the men, handled the rigging and thus regulated the amount of work done. The head logger told the hook tender to cut the output to five carloads per day. This was done and the result was that the men received eight hours' pay but did only four hours' actual work, yet the average wage per day is $6.00 to $7.50, the head logger receiving from $7.50 to $9.00 per day. He ordered the hook tender to cut the output. The hook tender was blamed for the delay. In this camp the cost of labour is 80 per cent.; cost of material, 20 per cent. By this sabotage the cost of producing lumber was all but doubled.

Mr. Forbes also said:

The most common practice is driving the railroad spike or bridge spike through the bark so it cannot be seen. This practice has occurred many times. It injures the machinery, as the band saw in the saw mills runs into the spike; it tears the teeth out and breaks the saw; oftentimes the tail sawyer is seriously injured or killed.

I may say in passing that the sawyer is seldom an I. W. W, when this accident occurs.

V. R. Lewis, of the Clear Lake Lumber Company, Clear Lake, Wash., made the following statement:

Wherever I.W.W.'s work they practise sabotage. At our plant at Clear Lake a Russian I.W.W. pulled the cotter pin out of the machine. This loosened the machinery, which was thrown with speed and force into the lake. The men jumped off barely in time to save their lives.

Another wobbley who arrived at the mill filled the waste we were burning for fuel with sand during the night. On the next day when the mill began operating the sand burned out the fire box. This held up the work until a new box could be secured.

Mr. Lewis says that he handles the labour situation in this manner: He gets 20 per cent, of married men in their organization; he pays them well and they live near the plant. They are the controlling factor, and when the I.W.W. agitators start to practise their teachings, the 20 per cent, take care of the I.W.W.'s, sometimes tarring and feathering them and driving them out of the camp. He adds:

The only way we can control the I.W.W.'s is by means of force. I have established social-welfare work and have tried to improve the environment of the men at my camp. I have a club house, a theatre, and a rooming house where clean beds can be obtained for one dollar per week. We have a baseball field where the men can play, and everything is done to provide wholesome, athletic, and clean amusement. This has increased the efficiency of the men, but has had no effect whatever on the agitators of the I.W.W.

Mr. Houston, of the Kent Lumber Company, said:

Our camp is not more than 30 miles from Seattle, and is near the city water shed. An I.W.W. named Miller was brakeman on our train, hauling lumber down a steep grade. Mr. Clark went with Miller on a few trips and cautioned him to be careful. When Miller went alone he did not set the brakes, but jumped off the car and let the carload of timber run downhill uncontrolled. This destroyed four thousand dollars' worth of property. Miller skipped the country without his clothes or suitcase. In searching through his belongings, full I.W.W. instructions were found in his suitcase, explaining exactly how to practise sabotage in the lumber camps.

Mr. Houston told of another instance. He said:

One crew of I.W.W.'s determined to strike, but before doing so hid away fifty boxes of our powder in one day. Soon a new crew started work and in felling a tree, it dropped on top of some of the powder, which exploded. Fortunately, no one was injured.

In the same connection Robert Allen, secretary of the Lumbermen's Association, said:

In all camps there is a fight over open and closed shops. Some plants insist on men joining the Loyal Legion of Loggers & Lumbermen, an association composed of employers and employees. Since the war many companies are trying to run an open shop and speed up output, but the wobbleys restrict the normal output to one half by their various methods of sabotage and agitation. The actual practice of sabotage, involving loss of life and property, has not been so prevalent the last year as it was in 1917 and the last of 1918 in the Northwest. This is because the employers and loyal working men use force when necessary to preserve the industry and protect property.

Following is an interview with George F. Russell, former postmaster of Seattle, now a member of the Employers' Association of Washington. He says:

The I.W.W. strike in the lumber industry in 1917, which hampered the securing of spruce for war needs, is the outstanding strike in that industry in the Northwest. Putting spikes in logs and tacking bark over same is a common practice of the I.W.W. Fires are started by placing phosphorus in wet papers and when it dries it sets fire to the timber by spontaneous combustion. Another way is to fill the ditch adjoining the railroad with small limbs of trees, covered with pitch, and as the train approaches they set fire to the dried brush and limbs and jump the train, and away they go. Another means of sabotage that has been used a great deal is putting emery dust or lemon juice in the ball bearings of saw-milling machinery. This destroys it in a few hours. In the fruit districts the I.W.W.'s put tacks in the trees; this stops the trees from bearing, and eventually kills them!

However, as there is no denial of the teaching and practice of sabotage by the I.W.W., the foregoing statements are sufficient to establish beyond a doubt the fact that it is used.

The I.W.W. publish and sing songs filled with sacrilege and hatred, songs reeking of the mire, glorifying crime, encouraging revolt, debauching the hearer, and ridiculing God and good, and all that is sweet and dear to true men and women everywhere.

In the I.W.W. Song Book published in Spokane is found the following advice:

You starving member of the unemployed: Why starve? We have produced enough. The warehouses are overflowing with the things we need. *Why starve?*

In other words, break into the warehouses! Take what you want!

Another motto runs: Labour is entitled to all it can take.

Another shining motto of the Song Book reads: Make it too expensive for the boss to take the lives and liberty of the workers. Stop the endless court trial by using the Wooden Shoe [Sabotage] on the job.

Extracts From I.W.W. Song Book

HARVEST WAR SONG

Chorus:

It's a long way, now understand me; it's a long way to town;
It's a long way across the prairie, and to Hell with Farmer John.
Up goes machine or wages, and the hours must come down;
For we're out for a winter's stake this summer, and we want no scabs around.

CHRISTIANS AT WAR

Onward, Christian soldiers! Duty's way is plain:
Slay your Christian neighbours, or by them be slain.
Pulpiteers are spouting effervescent swill.
God above is calling you to rob and rape and kill,
All your acts are sanctified by the Lamb on high;
If you love the Holy Ghost, go murder, pray and die.

Onward, Christian soldiers! Eat and drink your fill!
Rob with bloody fingers, Christ O.K.'s the bill.
Steal the farmers' savings, take their grain and meat;
Even though the children starve, the Saviour's bums must eat.
Bum the peasants' cottages, orphans leave bereft;
In Jehovah's holy name, wreak ruin right and left.

Onward, Christian soldiers! Drench the land with gore;
Mercy is a weakness all the gods abhor.
Bayonet the babies, jab the mothers, too;
Hoist the cross of Calvary to hallow all you do.
File your bullets' noses flat, poison every well;
God decrees your enemies must all go plumb to Hell.

Onward, Christian soldiers! Blighting all you meet.
Trampling human freedom under pious feet.
Praise the Lord whose dollar sign dupes his favourite race!
Make the foreign trash respect your bullion brand of grace.
Trust in mock salvation, serve as pirates' tools;
History will say of you: "That pack of God-damn fools."

Our country? The country of millions of hunted, homeless, hungry slaves! It is not OUR country.

THE PREACHER AND THE SLAVE

Long-haired preachers come out every night,
Try to tell you what's wrong and what's right;
But when asked 'bout something to eat
They answer with voices so sweet!

Chorus:

You will eat, bye and bye,
In that glorious land above the sky;
Work and pray, live on hay,
You'll get pie in the sky when you die.

And the starvation army may play.
And they sing and they clap and they pray.
Till they get all your coin on the drum.
Then they'll tell you when you're on the bum.

The I.W.W. hate all countries, but our country, being the freest country of all, is more hated and despised by them than all others combined. The I.W.W. ridicule the Divine law as well as human law. They believe it necessary and right to destroy all existing things. Their doctrine is that whatever is, is wrong. By a *minority rule,* founded on terrorism, they would change natural law, upset all man-made law, and — filled and obsessed by their ignorance — would teach the regeneration of society by upsetting everything that centuries of experience have taught us.

These men ridicule life and laugh at the earnest efforts of men whose lifetime toil has resulted in continuous, permanent advancement of the human race. They believe in the achievement of Paradise in a day — yes, in an hour! Force, violence, uproar — a continuous Donnybrook Fair — is their idea of progress! They are the hurry-up, get-it-over-quick boys, who have retarded the progress of the human race more than all the oppressors of the centuries!

They are against all government. They are against all morality. They are against all progress. They are against all decency. They preach no doctrine of construction and their policy of destruction is futile, weak, ignorantly vicious and ineffective. From Bakounin to Haywood they have taught every vile act, every despicable deed, to be right if it is done by one of their members.

Poisoning canned food by placing rodents in the cans, destroying vineyards, placing spikes in logs, burning mills, causing industrial accidents, forging checks — as they did in France; issuing false copies of the currency of different countries — as they do in Russia; all these things are holy in their sight! They look upon the government (the State) as an exhaustless mine from which each one may draw according to his desires.

Just what they expect to do after they secure control is a very-much-unknown, very-much-disagreed-upon, nebulous theory. They do know, however, that they want to use force, murder, violence, in order to overthrow society. They do agree that even though nine tenths of the people disagree with them, still they must, by might, establish an autocracy, and rule, or destroy the people themselves. They plan to establish a rule of the unfit, of the untrained, of the ignorant, of the unable, of the cruel, of the disappointed, and of the failures.

Of course, they talk only of proper distribution of the accumulated labour of the centuries now called wealth. They never talk of the production of any wealth by themselves, for themselves! That would mean work, toil, continued effort, brains, ability, honour, honesty, order. They look upon wealth as a static thing, as something already in existence, only needing proper division to bring about universal prosperity. Of course, they never consider that wealth is a constantly changing entity.

The stark truth stands out in all history that people do learn from experience, but only from their own experience. Those responsible for the momentous failures suffered by the workers always tell plain lies in order to excuse themselves. No better illustration of this can be had than the fake stories told

129

and written by the I.W.W.'s and their sympathizers after every defeat while their real story is an unbroken record of mistakes and failures.

Chapter Thirteen - Bolshevism in America; its Causes and Some Remedies

IN the preceding chapters I have told the story of syndicalism or I.W.W.'ism from its inception to the present day. It was entirely possible to have written several chapters on the Coeur d'Alène troubles, the Governor Steunenberg murder, the activities of the Western Federation of Miners, the San Francisco preparedness-parade horror, the Mooney case, and the Winnipeg general strike. This last general strike was simply a repetition of the Seattle strike. Our friend, James Duncan of Seattle, visited the Canadian cities and talked his plan of *"one big union"* before the Winnipeg strike occurred and after the attempted revolution in Seattle had failed. The Winnipeg strike lasted longer, but the end, as always, was a disastrous failure. Change the names, dates, etc., and the Winnipeg and Seattle affairs are almost identical. Let us now consider, in brief, the cause, effect, and possible means of cure of this great evil.

Our country to-day is confronted by a situation which threatens to destroy the very foundations of our government. It is not a time to "let things drift" or to hide our heads in the sand and say "all's well." In my judgment, American institutions are in greater danger to-day than at any previous time. The great World War called on us for men and goods, but in the main, our people, under the heat of conflict, stood together, worked together, fought together. Continued, persistent, and measurably successful efforts have been made, and are being made, to divide us on class lines. Sensible men can do naught else than consider the fundamental causes of the partial acceptance of this false gospel, and after finding the causes, consider the effects, search for the proper remedies, and if convinced that a cure has been found, unite as one and see to it that our institutions and our ideals do not perish from the earth.

If in the preceding chapters I have been able to convince the reader of our danger, I hope that in those which follow I shall be able to centre his best thought on solving the problems which must be solved, if we are to continue as in the past, a free, self-governing nation. With the fervent wish that this book may awaken the thinkers of the nation to a frank, free, and effective discussion of the questions involved which may result in their solution, I offer what are my beliefs in relation to them, realizing that there are thousands of men better fitted to perform the task set before me, and yet feeling that it is my duty as an American citizen to write what is in me.

When our Government was formed and our Constitution adopted, the plan was that the people of this country should rule this country; that no class, or clan, or organization of any kind should ever seize control and make of the United States of America any kind of government other than a government of, for, and by the people.

As time has swept on in its endless flight, the people of this nation, in legal and orderly manner, have changed the Constitution, and by amendment added to the fundamental law of the land those things which they, in their combined wisdom, considered necessary improvements. To this plan of continuous and neverending improvement all American citizens worthy of the name, and worthy of citizenship, have in the past and must in the future give undivided and unstinted support. But now, everywhere in this country, thousands refuse to abide by the orderly and legal procedure, time-honoured and century-tried, and advocate a reign of lawlessness and the overthrow of that government which to this date has functioned more successfully for *all the people* than any other yet devised and tried. We all realize that thousands are against our Government, but few of us have stopped to analyze the reasons why this is so.

Why, for instance, should a former slave from Russia, where poverty and oppression were his portion, desire to overthrow our Government, where he can, by simply complying with our naturalization laws, become one of the rulers himself, with no one else having a greater power than is vested in him through the sacred ballot?

Why should an American-born ridicule our Government, advocate its destruction, and work for the establishment of a "dictatorship" of any class whatever?

Why are so many educators more or less revolutionary in their beliefs?

What are the causes?

It is very easy to understand how the syndicalists of France in 1848 gained power. The Government repressed the workers and France was not a free, self-governed republic.

It is also easy, knowing of the previous centuries of misrule and tyranny in Russia, to understand the revolution there.

But the reasons for bolshevism in the United States are more complex and not so easy to define and understand. In my best judgment, the following are the major causes of this unrest and anarchy in our own country:

1st. Unassimilated aliens.
2nd. Ignorant Americans.
3rd. Increased cost of living.
4th. *Red* employers.
5th. Unthinking and dishonest adventurers and *Red* misleaders of labour.
6th. Oppression of governmental employees.
7th. Sickly sentimentalists.
8th. Discontented failures and delinquents.

It has been our proud boast that the United States holds wide open the portal to all who would live beneath our flag. With our enormous natural resources it has been repeatedly argued that no danger lurked in the easy admittance of the millions from foreign lands. To-day, however, men who give the subject of immigration even a cursory study must come to the conclusion that the *way has been made too easy, the path too broad, and the portal has been held too widely open for successful assimilation and digestion of the incoming alien.* There is a great deal of loose talk tending to go to the opposite extreme and close the door so that no one may enter. Either extreme, in my judgment, is just as wrong and dangerous as the other. To close the door entirely would bring manifold dangers and in time of need deprive this great nation of very valuable citizens. There are times when we need immigrants, and surely no American would want to close the door to those aspiring souls who want to escape from the thraldom and poverty of the Old World and become citizens and upbuilders in the New.

The time may come when our country will be fully developed, and when we shall have reached the point of saturation when no immigrants should be admitted, but that time is not yet here and will not come in your lifetime or mine. Is there no way that immigrants may be allowed to come when we need them and stopped when we do not need them? Is there no way that we can choose our future citizens from among the many applicants? Is there no way that these immigrants can be made real Americans and immediately apply for citizenship or be refused entrance?

I think there is, but it may be well, before I tell of my plan, to quote a few figures which are illuminating in relation to immigration. Since 1820 alone we have welcomed to our land more than thirty-four million immigrants and they came from the following countries:

5,500,000 from Germany	or 15% of total immigration
4,000,000 from Italy	" 12% " " "
4,000,000 from Austria-Hungary	" 12% " " "
3,300,000 from Russia	" 9%. " " "
2,130,000 from Scandinavia	" 6% " " "
8,200,000 from United Kingdom	" 24% " " "
775,000 from Canada	" 3% " " "
525,000 from France	" 2% " " "
352,000 from Greece	" 1% " " "
5,310,000 from all other countries	" 16% of total immigration
Total 34,092,000	100%

The immigrants from the United Kingdom were divided as follows: 60 per cent, came from Ireland, 33 per cent, from England, and the balance, or 7 per cent., from Scotland. The influence of the Scotch on our nation is far in excess of the relative percentage of immigration. One is amazed that so few could do so much, but the Scotch have always been famous for making a little go a long way.

It is of great interest to the student to know that our immigration in the main during and up to 1898 came from northwestern Europe and that our immigration since 1898 has come chiefly from southern Europe and Russia,

The following table illustrates the partial stoppage of the tide of immigration from northern Europe during the last few years and the increase in immigration from southern Europe during the same period:

Austria-Hungary from 1861 to 1898 (37 years) 1,170,000
Austria-Hungary from 1898 to 1914 (16 years) 2,875,000
Italy   from 1820 to 1898 (78 years)   700,000
Italy   from 1898 to 1914 (16 years) 3,300,000
Russia   from 1820 to 1898 (78 years)   645,000
Russia   from 1898 to 1914 (16 years) 2,610,000

You will note the enormous increase in immigration from Russia, Italy, and Austria-Hungary since 1898 and will probably *view with alarm* the decrease in the numbers from Great Britain and Scandinavia.

Another noticeable feature of our immigration is the fact that of all the millions who came between and including the years 1900 and 1912, seventy out of every hundred were males. For every female, therefore, came more than twice as many males. This apparently definitely establishes the fact that only a small percentage of *family immigration* has taken place since the year 1900. In searching the immigration reports, one finds that the percentage of females coming to this country prior to 1900 was very much greater than since that time. Therefore, we may say that immigration has increased from southern Europe and Russia, and decreased from northern Europe, and that male immigration has increased and female immigration decreased in proportion as the source has changed.

In the years immediately following the Civil War whole families emigrated from Europe, mostly from northern Europe, while to-day very few families come to the United States in comparison. We are to-day welcoming, principally from Russia and southern Europe, single men, and not families. In the years following the Civil War the foreign born were rapidly assimilated because of their comparative fewness in each community; because the alien's family came with him; because the children of the alien were always a great factor in inculcating our American ideals in their parents; and because *he usually went out on the land and tilled the soil,* established a family, took out his citizenship papers, acquired a farm, and became a *real American.* To-day, as a general thing, he does not go out on the land; he does not have a family; he does not establish a home, but herds in congested, foreign colonies in our great cities; and hence does not become Americanized as readily or as rapidly. Oft-times he becomes an itinerant and wanders from place to place. These are facts which must be considered in solving the immigration problem *which is part and parcel of our bolshevik menace.*

The irreconcilable agitating alien, bolshevik or anarchist, should not be allowed to remain one hour longer than is necessary to go through the proper legal forms to send him back to the land from which he came. He is an ever-increasing danger, is no good to himself or any one else, is a trouble breeder, a teacher of falsehood and sedition, and *must, and shall, be sent out of this land of the free.*

The American people want no further trifling with these men. If there are not sufficient laws quickly and inexpensively to deport these people, Congress should enact them, and any president who would veto such necessary and just measures would and should be impeached. This matter could easily be handled and no further comment is necessary. The alien who has not taken any steps to become a citizen should at once be asked what his intentions are, and if he shows no disposition to Americanize himself, he also should be sent back. *Let them either become Americans or go home.*

Every facility should be provided to enable the aliens already here to assimilate our ideals. In every portion of our land community centres should be established and aliens compelled to attend them until they have learned our language and understand, at least in some measure, the meaning of our institutions. The school houses should be used every evening for classes of prospective citizens. The state can well afford to furnish teachers for our future citizens. In the hotel and lodging-house districts schools and libraries should be established, if necessary with sawdust on the floor, where entertainments, moving-picture shows, instructive lectures, etc., depicting American history, can be given.

One of the great troubles in our cities in the West, where the saloon has gone out, is that there absolutely is no social centre for itinerant workers. When the saloons were closed a great I.W.W. hall was opened in Seattle, where the workmen were made to feel at home and many became converts. It is all right to close the saloon, but it is not all right to fail to replace the saloon, which had one merit: it provided a loafing and lounging place where men could meet their fellows. Why not open up places where men can *pay for what they get, but enjoy themselves in their own way as long as they keep the peace?* In some places religious people have opened missions, but the religious atmosphere drives many men away. The average man wants leisure to do as he wishes, not as someone tells him. Recreational, social, and educational features could easily be coordinated and provided.

The lodging-house districts of most cities ought to be burned to the ground and rebuilt with new, modem, sanitary buildings, having in them pool rooms, billiard halls, bowling alleys, libraries, baths, etc. Some day when you have time, dear reader, visit your own lodging-house district and see for yourself if I am not right. The peculiar part of this proposition is that any such buildings will be self-sustaining and show a good interest on the investment. Build a few clean, sanitary places in which men may live, sleep, learn, and enjoy life. Every possible effort must be made to train the alien in his new duties as well as his new privileges. Almost everyone knows what their rights are, but few realize that without duties well performed our rights would soon cease to be.

One of the greatest hindrances to the Americanization of aliens is the fact that during the past years so many thousands have herded together and established foreign centres or colonies in our great cities. I have visited these foreign settlements, and conditions are unspeakable. One would not believe how many of these people live, herded together in crowded tenements, with only the pavement for playgrounds for their children, with the foreign-language press read almost exclusively, and with foreign modes of life and foreign methods of thinking prevailing almost exclusively. Not only are these districts a menace to our Government, but they are immensely harmful to the immigrants themselves. The tendency to herd together in the great cities often deprives our country of the benefit of the training of generations across the sea. Many, many thousands of these folk are farmers from the country districts of Europe. Under our present system or lack of system we allow them to gather in the slum districts of our cities and we make poor sweat-shop tailors, etc., of men who know how to raise food and would, if given the opportunity, continue the work with which they are familiar. It is probably the most foolish thing we could do with this human material. Is there a constructive, common-sense method of solving the problems of Americanization and immigration? I think there is, and submit that selective immigration and scientific distribution of aliens can be worked out without any particular shock and without any particular effort or expense, to the lasting benefit of the immigrant as well as to our country.

In days gone by we have admitted, in the main, those who had the fare to get here and wanted to come. It seems to me that in the future we should admit only those who want to come to this country and become real American citizens, and, of these, those only *that we have need for.*

In other words, let us select our future citizens. How can this be done? Very easily. In every country across the sea we have representatives. Let the intending emigrant call upon one of our agents in Europe and make application for entrance; let him deposit with our representative $25 or $50 or whatever is necessary; let the aspirant be at once physically and mentally examined; let him fill out a questionnaire somewhat similar to the one our boys filled out for the army, giving his previous occupation, training, and history. Upon the examination being completed and the investigation made, our representative should send full particulars to a board of immigration in Washington, D.C. This board would then become a clearing house for immigrants, and its main duty would be to select only those who are fit to partake of our privileges and *fit and willing to perform the duties of citizenship.* The applicant should also be asked to signify his desire in relation to his destination or future home.

These applications and reports would come to our national clearing house for prospective citizens and the board should have *final and complete authority as to the destination* of the alien. Many good farmers would, no doubt, signify their desire to remain in New York. This should not be allowed. The farmer should go to that part of the United States where his particular ability can be best used and where men of his training are needed. No one, under any circumstance, should be admitted who is not willing to work. The board could very easily prevent the formation or future growth of foreign colonies by simply refusing to allow the alien to go to that district where his unassimilated brethren live. Until the immigrant has become an American citizen, he should not be allowed to go to or live in any part of the country he desires; he should to a greater or less degree be under the supervision and direction of our authorities; he should be registered and kept track of and aided during his five-year period of probation before he becomes a citizen.

This board of immigration would of necessity have to have a definite and reasonably accurate knowledge of the need of men in the different parts of the United States, and the immigrants should be sent to fill those needs and for no other reason. There would be years, perhaps, when not one single mechanic was needed. During those years mechanics would not be selected.

It seems to me that the greatest problem of our country is to get people on the land and stop, in a measure, the overgrowth of our cities. We have become a great industrial nation, but our farming development is not keeping pace with our industrial growth. Why not select men who are farmers, preferably men with families, and send them to that part of the country in need of farmers? By doing so we increase our supply of food, clothing, etc., and reduce the cost of living for all, including the folks in the great cities. Manufacturing, etc., can only become established on a firm basis when we produce sufficient of the necessities of life to take care of the men engaged in industry. It is not lack of land that stops our agricultural production. It is lack of sufficient and efficient man power. We have two billion acres of land and only one in seven is under cultivation. All over the West and South millions of arable acres lie idle, awaiting only the hand of the husbandman to make them "blossom like the rose." Irrigation of arid lands in our country is as yet in its infancy. There are millions of acres of land that need diking, draining, and clearing. We also have a great many millions of acres already prepared that are only partially cultivated because of lack of farm help. It does seem to me that we need, more than anything else, the immigrant farmer, who wants to become a citizen and knows how to farm. This selective system, with proper distribution, it seems to me would solve the problem of the immigrant. It would make it better for us and better for him. He would go into a farming community that needs him; he would find useful remunerative employment; he would become Americanized in a short time, and *he would help feed us all.* The man who raises food is seldom a bolshevist.

While the alien has given us a great deal of trouble, he is not the only trouble-maker in our country. The American born who does not understand the principles of our Government has, oft-times, joined the alien agitator in trying to destroy our nation, and in my judgment a good deal of this unrest has been our own fault. We have, in the main, neglected the *Americanization of Americans.* While our census report shows a comparatively small percentage of illiteracy, the army reports, compiled after men were selected for service, tell a very different story. In the census report men and women were marked "Literate" if they were able to write their names. Thousands had learned to write their names who were unable to read and understand the ordinary articles appearing in the daily press. This condition was a revelation to many of us, who fatuously believed the story told by the census. The laws for the compulsory education of children should and must be rigidly enforced. The most ignoble work of man is an uneducated child. The lack of proper preparation in youth not only injures the child, but weakens our whole national fabric. No chain is stronger than its weakest link, and a great country must have a great people behind it. Someone said: "You cannot make an A1 army out of C4 men." This is as true of every other walk in life.

By "education" I do not mean "schooling" only — I mean training in useful and needed occupations. The high-school graduate cannot claim to be "educated," even though he stood at the head of his class, if he is *unable to do useful, necessary work in the world.* No man can say he is an educated man if he is not familiar with the ordinary common-sense laws of keeping well, of sanitation, of hygiene, etc. Certainly no man can consider himself "fit" unless he knows how to do at least one thing for which the *world will pay enough to give him a living.*

We must properly train our children in the homes first, and then see to it that the necessary things of life are taught in our schools. Men must be able to contribute something useful to society in order to be an asset instead of a liability. Without proper home and school training many men become leaners instead of lifters. Without proper knowledge of the fundamentals of our Government, many men live their lives out without really appreciating what a great, self-governing, free country America is.

I believe it is as important to have a Department of Education established and its head given a place in the President's Cabinet as it is to have an Agricultural or a War Department. I know of no reason why a Department of Public Health also should not be created. Health and education are certainly primary requisites for a people such as ours. The monetary expense involved would be returned a thousand fold in a better and more fit citizenship.

Americanism should be a regular course in all schools, just the same as arithmetic and grammar. It is the very warp and woof of our civilization. Surely it is important — essential. I would rather have my children understand the history and ideals of our country than that they learn Latin or Greek. I contend that no unbiased, unprejudiced person can sincerely advocate the overthrow of this Government if he understands just what kind of a government it is. There are so many false teachers of soap-bubble Utopias that it is well that, right at the start, the children should be taught Americanism and also be shown the fallacy and successive and universal failure of the quack cure-alls that are ever and anon offered to the gullible.

During the past few years there has been a seemingly never-ending increase in the cost of the necessities of life. According to Bradstreet, the increase in cost of living from 1914 to 1918 was 119 per cent., the United

States Bureau of Labour makes it 103 per cent., and Dun 94 per cent. From carefully prepared data we found in fixing the salaries of city employees that the increase from July 1, 1918, to July 1, 1919, was 12½ per cent.

While this increase has been followed by increased wage scales, it is unquestionably a fact that the increase in wages has not in a great many instances kept pace with the increased cost of living. Restricted production has, in many instances, increased the cost of production and thus has increased the cost of living. From personal observation and from accurate first-hand knowledge I can say that in the lumber industry the same crew of men in Washington do not produce more than 60 to 65 per cent, as much in the same length of time as did those same workers a few years ago, and yet the wages measured in food, clothing, etc., of the men have been increased, in many instances nearly doubled.

The fact that all who would work could find work, that there was a shortage of men, that employers had to keep those they had or get at least as bad a crew, or possibly worse, has militated against efficiency amongst the workers. The sabotage and restricted output were never more apparent than at the present time. When enterprises are confronted with a steadily increasing wage scale and at the same time with a continuous decrease in production, it naturally becomes more and more difficult to conduct them successfully.

However, the complaint of high costs has just grounds and the profiteer has raised many articles of daily need to unconscionable heights. The dissatisfaction caused thereby has made many otherwise perfectly normal people place the entire blame upon our Government. The fact that the World War and its needs called from productive enterprises millions of men and consumed billions of days of labour is given small thought. The great taxes made necessary by the war have simply caused the dealer and manufacturer to transfer this extra cost to his goods; and when wages are increased, he tries as far as possible to do the same thing.

The arrest and punishment of the *profiteers* seems to me to be only scratching the surface. To me it seems that the fundamental and sensible way to stop the ever-increasing cost is to deflate the currency and increase the production of goods. On July 1, 1914, we had $33.96 per capita circulating medium. On July 1, 1918, we had $54.28 per capita circulating medium.

The following statement taken from that very valuable farm paper, *Capper's Weekly*, of September 13, 1919, is certainly interesting:

MONEY AND CREDIT AS A CAUSE OF HIGH PRICES: OUR CURRENCY INFLATION ABOUT 60 PER CENT.

Inflation of currency and credit is held to be chiefly responsible for high prices by economists. A subscriber of the National Republican discovers that the stocks of money in the United States have increased two thirds in the last five years. In other words, currency has increased about 60 per cent, or from $33.96 to $54.28 per capita while living has risen 70 to 94 per cent.

The statement of the Secretary of the Treasury, issued July 1st, gives a summary of the amount of money in circulation in the United States on July 1, 1914 and July 1, 1919. It is as follows:

KIND OF MONEY	1914	1919
Gold Coin (inc. Bullion in Treas.)	$ 614,321,674	$1,172,953,529
Gold Certificates	1,035,454,129	542,214,728
Standard Silver Dollars . . .	70,314,176	81,576,350
Silver Certificates	479,452,376	169,939,003
Subsidiary Silver	160,263,675	232,147,836
Treasury Notes of 1890 . . .	2,427,038	1,745,230
United States Notes (Greenbacks)	338,839,637	332,938,544
National Bank Notes. . . .	718,085,637	659,831,150
Federal Reserve Bank Notes. .		163,682,696
Federal Reserve Notes . . .		2,493,902,462
Totals	$3,419,158,342	$5,850,931,528
Amount per capita	33.96	54.28

It will be seen that while the stock of gold coin and bullion increased $558,631,855, the amount of gold certificates (based on gold in the Treasury not included in above) decreased $493,232,401, leaving a net increase of only $65,399,454, in spite of the large importations of gold from Europe in the early part of the war — before we entered it.

The stock of silver decreased $126,367,038.

Greenbacks decreased $5,901,099, and national bank notes, $68,254,487, as both these issues are being gradually retired.

The Federal Reserve and Federal Reserve Bank notes — all issued since 1914 — amount to $2,582,629,572, making a net increase of money in circulation during the five years of $2,461,858,214.

But the paper money increased $2,582,629,572, while the metal money decreased $120,771,358. The per capita increased from $33.96 to $54.28, or $20.32, being about 60 per cent.

It seems to me, however, that the above statement but partially covers our inflation. The different series of bonds issued for war purposes amounted to $19,086,000,000). To a greater or less degree these bonds, especially in the smaller denominations, are being used as currency. Go to a ladies' suit emporium and sit in the salesroom for a couple of hours, and I am sure you will find that the bonds are being traded for merchandise at their market value in many instances. I have known of several large real-estate transactions, and dozens of small ones, where bonds were used as currency; $19,086,000,000 of bonds were issued. Now let us suppose that 20 per cent, of the bonds issued are used for such purposes and circulate as money. That means that instead of the total of $5,841,026,582 of circulating medium we have an increased amount of $3,817,200,000 to add to it, making a grand total of $9,658,226,582, or a per-capita circulating medium of nearly $90. It may be that only 10 per cent, of bonds are used as currency; if so, the per-capita circulation would be more than $70. Gradual deflation of the currency will gradually decrease the price of goods, and gradually reduce the cost of living. During the readjustment period many business bubbles will be pricked, but honest enterprise and industry will be benefited.

Unless there be a gradual and continuous deflation of the currency by the powers that be, it does seem that one of these days the top will blow off the tea kettle and bring immediate and disastrous results. I am convinced that the American people do not want an embargo or restriction of output placed on goods going across the sea to people who are really working and trying to adjust themselves. I am just as firmly convinced, however, that the American people strenuously object to going without themselves or paying exorbitant prices for needful things, if these articles are to go to people who refuse to work and do for themselves. We are perfectly willing to be a Christmas tree, but we want the presents to go to those who are trying and not to those who are loafing. Prompt and effectual action in relation to these matters will make the ground less receptive for the planting of bolshevism, as well as other isms.

One of the fruitful causes of hatred and discontent is the *Red* employer of labour. He is as dangerous to the employers as to the rest of the national fabric. *Red* employers are a constant menace, and upon their deeds and their words many an agitator has hung a convincing sermon. You know some of them and so do I. We should be very thankful that every day they become less and soon will be an inconsequential minority in the land. These men are cave dwellers, as far as modem industry is concerned. Some of them still look upon the workers as merely machines to be used, and then scrapped. In many places workers are compelled to toil in unsanitary factories with defective lighting and ventilation systems, and every improvement of their lot comes only after a hard struggle, occasioning loss to all society. I am thankful to say that *Red* employers are few in number and that during the Victory Loan trip I made throughout the country, I found that progressive, decent employers of labour condemned their actions as vigorously as did the workers themselves. The factories universally must be places where men and women can do their work without loss of health and vigour. The worker's capital is his health, his eyesight, his physical and mental fitness. Living conditions must be such that the worker can go to his work singing, "My Country 'Tis of Thee, Sweet Land of Liberty," and mean it. Light, healthful surroundings cut down industrial accidents and increase production. Such conditions are not only morally right, but from the standpoint of efficiency, essential. I have carefully read the reports of production of the same men in the same factories under bad conditions and good conditions, and these reports were a revelation to me. Men produce more goods and better goods when conditions are right. These are proven facts, and easily demonstrable. It gave me a great deal of confidence in the honest intention of the great majority of employers to listen for hours to reports and surveys of the conditions of their employees. It also made one feel he was in America when he saw careless employers called up on the carpet by fellow employers and practically commanded to install certain badly needed improvements.

All this cannot be done in a day, but it can and must be done. The people who can get it done the quickest are the men engaged in similar undertakings. The facts properly presented will cause any one but a feebleminded employer to remedy such conditions. It cannot be too often emphasized that it does not pay, even in a financial way, to have anything but the best living conditions in one's factory. It is true that laws are on the books and oft-times enforced, but *there should be no need of calling on the law to compel the employer to make the necessary and righteous improvements about his plant.* The real man does right cheerfully and willingly as soon as the faults are called to his attention. The other kind of a man should be compelled to do likewise.

In every organization, large or small, be it church, lodge, labour union, or otherwise, there is always a small minority who look at all things from a purely selfish standpoint. Whenever an organization is started, the pay-roll parasite is always present. The professional agitator is usually as dishonest as the Devil, and just as unscrupulous. He gets his salary every week, strike or no strike, trouble or peace. He is always trying to figure out some way of bringing about friction between the employer and the employees. The louder he talks, the less he does; the more he promises, the more likely he is to be followed and believed. I have had a great deal of experience with this breed who never do any work themselves, but work the workers. They plan trouble and oft-times bring it about. They preach class hatred, antagonism, and destruction all the time. They have cost the workers of this country more than all the *Red employers* in Christendom. They care not what happens to the workmen or to the employer as long as they sit tight in their places of power. They are not leaders — they are misleaders. They do not want better conditions or better wages, but continually preach taking control of all things. Sometimes an employer is in the midst of his busiest season; he must get out his product in order to pay his obligations and exist. The workers are receiving a fair day's wage for a fair day's work. This is such a man's opportunity. He gradually insinuates the idea into the minds of the men that if they *strike right then the employer can he held up and made to pay a greater wage than his competitor;* that he will go bankrupt if his doors close. Sometimes the men strike and win, oft-times they strike and lose, but in the end, they always lose when engaged in such undertakings.

The labour question is not a one-sided affair. The *Red employer* is bad, but the *Red employee* is just as despicable. As I have said before in this book, they are interchangeable anarchists. Labour must purge itself of these Red leaders, even as the employers must cleanse themselves of their Red associates; otherwise — no peace, no progress. The Red labour leaders make the workmen believe that Utopia is just a week ahead. The progressive and constructive labour leader preaches steady and never-ceasing progress. He knows that progress comes by evolution and not by revolution. He plays the game, is true to his fellows, but does not impoverish his followers by advising them to make impossible and unjust demands. In the long run, he leads Labour to greater heights, better conditions, and more prosperity. The Red misleader befools the workers for a while, but some day they throw him out, bag and baggage. He then changes his location and starts the same thing over again. Progressive employers should blacklist the Reds among them, and decent Labour should drive them out of their unions as they will certainly destroy their organizations if allowed to remain.

I want to impress this thought upon the reader, be he employer or employee. In enterprise there are but four elements essential to success:

First: Well-paid labour.

Second: Equally well-paid administration.

Third: Equally well-paid capital.

Fourth: Consideration and justice for the ultimate consumer.

Capital must receive a reasonable reward or it shrinks into hiding. Administrative heads must be well paid or they lose interest, initiative, and efficiency. Labour must be satisfied, must have good living conditions, and must receive the highest possible remuneration. The dark, noisome factories *must be torn down* and replaced by new buildings where the sunlight of heaven pours in on the workers. The worker's precious eyesight must be saved. His fingers, his legs, his life must be protected from injury by every possible safety device. His food and housing conditions must be excellent. His children must be well fed and well clothed and well educated. The administrative heads must not only be careful that Capital receives dividends, but must be careful to see to it that Labour receives its just reward, and the *shareholders must not only take interest in their annual dividends, but in the workmen and the plant itself.*

The workmen must take an interest in their work and in the success of the enterprise. They must do a full day's work for a full day's pay. They must be fair with their employer, and their organization must either play square and *keep its contracts* or it will be destroyed. No wrong thing can long stand! Any organization advocating wrong must pass away. The only manner in which Labour can win, hold lasting respect, and maintain itself, is by being respectable and *keeping its word.* Cooperation in industry is absolutely essential. The thing which hurts the enterprise hurts all engaged in that enterprise. The burning down of a mill in the forests of Washington makes everyone in the world just that much poorer. The slowing up of one man adds to the poverty of the whole.

The agitation of unthinking and dishonest adventurers in all walks of life will probably always go on in a greater or lesser degree. Without the fibre to be successful themselves, they hate all success. With nothing at stake, they try to disaffect those who have everything at stake. Without the power of thought, many of them have good memories and are oft-times able to recite the catch words and phrases in common use. They have no desire for progress or plan for its achievement. They are simply passengers who refuse to shovel coal under the boilers, refuse to do the work they can do, and are incapable of doing the more important things necessary to the successful voyage. They are passengers who pay no fare. They eat, are clothed and cared for, but do not pay for what they eat, wear, or enjoy. Purely parasitic and entirely selfish, they make a certain amount of trouble for all decent people. They may be called the camp-followers that follow the army but neither fight at the front nor work in the rear. Many of them are vagrants, pure and simple, although some of them are well-dressed. However, their loose words fall on barren soil if the workers, employees and employers, cooperate and work together, and unless all do work together for the common good, industrial success and progress must cease to be. The sooner we all realize this, the better.

For a long time past the interests of the employee and the employer have been the only ones considered. The employer says: "I must have so much," and the employee says: "I must have so much." Seldom does either take into consideration the ultimate consumer upon whom they both live. The other party — the public in general — should be taken into consideration. Time after time I have seen labour troubles settled between the employer and the employees without any consideration whatsoever given to the public. For instance, the coal miners decide that they want $1.00 more per day. Their employer assents and promptly adds the dollar, or more, to the cost of coal that we - you and I - use in our homes. When the great middle class in this country are awakened to the fact that their rights are not protected, they will, as they should, have a part and a voice in the settlement of all future disputes.

Many of us seem to believe that poor pay and bad working conditions are the result of private business enterprise run for profit. In all the arguments for municipal and governmental ownership the first premise is that the workers will toil under ideal conditions and receive absolutely fair and square treatment and just recompense. Government-owned and government-conducted enterprises are nm for service and not for profit. Belonging to all of us, it is ridiculous that all should be overcharged in order to show a great profit, which would be returned in some form to us all. Therefore, it has been argued that there is no incentive for underpaying the employee in such enterprises. There being no incentive to make profit out of the work of the workers, in the nature of things the workmen will be better cared for and his rights more fully protected than in industries under private ownership and control.

Strange as it may seem, it has not worked out that way in all instances. I desire to state that it is my belief that a private employer would be tarred and feathered and driven from the community in which he lived if he underpaid so persistently any class of men and women in his employ as do our school boards, for instance, the teachers, or our colleges their professors. We have seen how the great hatred that the workmen first felt for the machine that they believed would deprive them of the right to work was transferred within a short time to the owner of the machine, the employer. The employer who does not treat his men right is sure to reap eventually his just reward.

There can be no escape from this condition. Men who are robbed and oppressed will feel resentment and use every artifice to "get back" at the employer who is responsible. When a governmental body mistreats or underpays its employees, the employees turn their resentment against the responsible body, which, in this instance, is the State itself. In other words, if the Government does not do right by those whom it employs, they grow to feel that the Government is a bad government and *should he changed*. If this is true, we should expect to find upon investigation that many of our Government's underpaid workers would adopt some ism or other in the hope of a change and a consequent improvement in their lot. This seems reasonable, does it not? It is natural, is it not? Let us consider the actual situation for a moment.

The teaching class in this country numbers more than 750,000 men and women, principally *women.* They are recruited from all walks of life, but come principally from that great middle class which, in the final analysis, directs the destinies of our nation. The teaching class has, in times past, been recognized by all *thoughtful people* as the mainstay, as the bulwark of our nation. Thousands of speeches have been made, and thousands of chapters have been written, painting the glory of the "little red school house on the hill." Of course the school house is but a building of lath and boards and brick and plaster. The spirit of the school house is the teacher. Without the teacher, the school house is a dead thing. The teacher is IT, not the building. All right, what have we done with and for our school teacher?

Last fall twenty-five million big and little children packed up their books and slates and pencils and filled the thousands of school houses throughout the land. They were your children and my children. We had done our best at home to inculcate decency, patriotism, and love of country in their hearts and minds, but when school started, with no misgivings we turned these twenty-five million boys and girls over to the teachers. They were to mould their opinions, their ideas, their lives. They were to teach the good and see to it that the bad entered not into the young minds.

Roosevelt said:

You teachers make the whole world your debtor; and of you it can be said if you did not do your work well, this Republic would not outlast the span of a generation.

We have all repeated time and again: "Knowledge is Power." We have, in a desultory way, spoken well of the school teacher, who lays the first foundation for knowledge and right thinking. We all realize the gravity, the supreme importance of the teacher's duty. The teacher's personality, training, and professional habits are and always have been typical of our best middleclass Americans. The teacher's place is not only useful, it is necessary, of supreme and vital importance. Again I ask you fellow American citizens: "How have you treated the teachers?" We admit our very existence depends upon them; that our children are turned over to them for character building, and that on

144

the nature of their work rests, very largely, the nature of the pupil's usefulness in after life. One great organization has said:

Give us the child in the formative period of life and we defy you to shake our teachings in the years thereafter.

Being such an important part of our civilization, of course we have seen to it that the school teachers are respected, happy, and well paid, and that teaching offers to the youth a career in life second to none. Of course we would not oppress or underpay such valuable members of society. We — you and I — have, of course, seen to it that our educators are so well treated that they radiate love of country and patriotism and feel that this Government — their Government — our Government — is treating them as they should be treated. Of course, we have done no such thing! As a rule, they leave the classroom as students, only to reenter as teachers. Their cloistered life tends to preserve unsullied the high and conservative principles of thought, character, and action which they pass on to the children in their charge. Their birth, breeding, and daily habits naturally make them the conservative exponents of the established order of things in government, society, and industrial comity. They should be consistent upholders of American law, order, and ideals, the strongest bulwark of the nation against radicalism and unrest. They should be apostles of evolutionary progress instead of revolutionary destruction. They should be the democratic servants of us all in the making of our future American citizenry.

The American of to-morrow — perhaps the world of to-morrow — will be the product of the American teachers of to-day.

How have we, you and I, cared for our teachers and educators?
It is time to answer — time to confess.
The average daily wage of the American teacher in 1918 was $1.48 per day. The average daily wage of the American school teacher in 1919 was $1.63 per day. The National Educational Association shows that our best-paid teachers in 320 of our largest American cities in 1918 received the following magnificent annual salaries:

Median salary for 59,020 teachers, elementary city schools, $818.19
Median salary for 3,779 teachers, intermediate city schools, $899.42
Median salary for 13,976 teachers, high schools,
$1,249.50

There are 19,017 teachers, including 338 high school teachers, in city schools, who receive less than $700 per year.
There are 2,931, including 33 high school teachers, in city schools, *who receive less than 500 dollars per year.*
No, these are not statistics from the year 1818, but are figures gathered for the year 1918!

145

The Railway Wage Commission in 1919 urged that the lowest-paid railroad man should receive *at least* $1,400.

The U.S. Navy Yard blacksmith received in 1918 $2,396; electricians, $2,321; *labourers,* $1,297; and *char-women,* $873.

The Johnson-Nolan Act provided that the minimum wage of all civil-service employees of the United States, including *watchmen, janitors,* and *scrub women should be raised to* $1,080 a year.

Director-General McAdoo authorized increases to railway employees amounting to 300 million or more per year *and said a man could not maintain efficiency on an income of less than $1,400 per year.*

Other Government employees within the past few years have been raised 40 to 60 per cent.

Teachers have been raised in the same period from 10 to 12 per cent.

In Illinois in 1918, when 300 teachers received less than $400 *per year,* the average monthly salary of 15 miners was $217.78. The average monthly salary of 15 teachers was $55.

An Austrian alien miner was paid more than $2,700 in wages for the year 1918, while the principal of the high school in the same town, an American woman, with a university degree, *received only* $765.

"Knowledge is Power."

In Raleigh, North Carolina, there appeared in the *News and Observer* of January 13, 1919, two want ads. One was for a coloured barber at $25 per week with a possible increase to $35. The other read:

Wanted:- Teacher of Latin for the Lumberton High School. Salary $70 a month.

"Knowledge is Power."

In Washington, D. C, the Senate succeeded in the last session in raising the minimum salary of teachers in the District of Columbia to the level of the dog catchers. It had been $500, but was raised to $750 with an established *maximum* of $1,300 to be reached *after twenty-five years of service.*

In our national capital and the seat of the Federal Bureau of Education one third of the teachers receive less than $1,000 per year. Many millions are spent at our national capital, and rightly so, to study methods to improve the breed of swine, horses, and cattle, but the school teachers must teach twenty-five years in order to get less money than the street labourer, less money than the Greek waiter at the hotel, less than the bootblack or porter in the barber shop.

In New York the teacher's pay is less than that of the street sweeper while in Baltimore the teachers have earnestly pleaded that their recompense be made equal to that of the keeper of the monkey house in the Zoological Gardens.

In Pennsylvania the teachers petitioned the Legislature to raise their minimum group to $60 per month, those with normal-school certificates to $75, the next group to $85, and the highest group, including principals and superintendents, to a level of from 10 to 20 per cent, more than they have been receiving.

While this campaign was going on, the following ad. was appearing in Philadelphia papers:

Pile drivers and carpenters wanted. Pay 85 cents per hour; double pay for overtime and triple pay for Sunday.

In one western city the school teachers ran in debt to a local bank in order to purchase Liberty Bonds. When they asked for an increase in their wage, they were told:

You don't need an increase. You were able to buy Liberty Bonds.

Once again I want to call the reader's attention to the fact that the increased cost of living during the past few years was, according to Bradstreet, 119 per cent.; Dun, 94 per cent.; and the United States Department of Labour, 103 per cent.

The increased cost of living has cut the teachers' wages more than 60 per cent., since 1914, up to July 1, 1918, and 12½ per cent, since that time and up to this writing.

The wages for teachers before the war were disgraceful. The average for the nation at large was but $543.31, while in twenty-three states the average was even less.

The percentage of men teachers in the schools has declined from 42.8 per cent, in 1880 to 19.6 per cent, in 1914, and the percentage is much less now.

During the World War doctors, dentists, and engineers were given commissions. Teachers were allowed to serve in reconstruction and educational work *but only as privates.*

Is Knowledge Power?

I think the above proves that we have been degrading and robbing the educators of this nation. Let the United States Steel Company treat their employees as badly, and there would be a Congressional investigation, and someone would either leave the country or go to jail. I think it clear that the teachers feel a just and righteous resentment because of their treatment. They feel their employers have not treated them fairly. They don't guess about it, they know; and you and I know that it is a damnable, inexcusable outrage. We have paid them so little that many who could leave the profession have left it. There is no career, present or future, for the educators of our children. Their resentment is growing daily.

A person takes his station in life very largely on an economic basis. The school teacher who receives such a pittance cannot associate with her equals in training, intelligence, or breeding, she is more or less of an outcast. While the carpenter takes his car and goes for a drive on Sunday she takes long hikes through the country, but of late she has not even been able to do this — shoe leather costs too much.

147

The employer of the school teacher is, in the great majority of cases, a governmental body. The school teachers' resentment has been and is directed at the employer. Many men have wondered: "Why is it that so many teachers and educators believe in this or that ism? Why are so many of them antagonistic to existing government?" The manner in which we have treated them is the answer, and *this resentment, sometimes unconsciously, is being passed on to the children and youth of this nation every day in every state in this land.*

Forget, if you will, the 750,000 teachers, but remember the twenty-five million children and remember our national ideals. Can they continue if the teaching body becomes more and more resentful and instills more and more of the virus of unrest into the growing minds of our little ones? Either the teachers are entitled to enough to live on in decency and comfort or they are unfit to use our magnificent school buildings and have charge of the training of our youth. Either their pay must be increased to meet at least their pre-war earnings, which were far too low, or we are criminal exploiters of labour — the worst kind of *Red employers*.

Forget the pay-envelope end of the question for a moment, and let us consider the effect on the children. We teach the children that *"Knowledge is Power,"* and yet the disseminators of knowledge get less than the bootblack who polishes their shoes, a good deal less than the street-car man who collects their nickel, and less than the newsboy who has a stand on the corner!

The dissatisfied educator is the most dangerous individual in our midst. Let us see to it, you and me, at once, that the educators in our locality get their just dues. Let us treat them in such a manner that they will have reason to love our country and teach its beneficent doctrines. Let us be fair and square, and if our present school board is still pre-Adamite, *get rid of it.* Run yourself if necessary and make the teacher's pay the issue, and I am sure the people will rally to your support. Treat the educator as he should be treated, as an honoured, necessary servant of the whole people, doing incalculable good and intrusted with the future destinies of this Republic. If you paid your chauffeur who cares for your car as little as you pay the educator for caring for your children, what would happen?

It is not my purpose to discuss in detail, or at great length, the inadequate and insufficient wages received by many of our government employees, but I desire in brief to call the attention of the reader to the past and present condition of the postal employees of the United States. In 1913 the following was the wage scale paid by the United States Government:

$800.00 to $1,200.00 per year for clerks and carriers. Since that time their pay has been slightly increased, and is now; $1,000.00 per year on entering the service with a maximum, to be reached after six years' service, of $1,500.00.

But even now it is entirely too low when compared with the cost of living, the newer employees receiving a wage less than the Director-General of Railroads said was necessary to maintain efficiency. These workers perform an essential and important task, and yet their pay does not now average as much as the pay of the day labourer throughout the United States. It were better for us to pay a little more postage, if necessary, than to underpay the employees of this Department.

An evening paper lies before me and I find a report stating that the "morale" of the Pacific Fleet is at a very low ebb; that a great many officers have resigned, and that a great many more are trying to have their resignations accepted in order that they may return to private life and enter into some employment where they can support their families. Secretary of the Navy Josephus Daniels, is reported as saying that some of the best men in the United States Navy have pleaded and begged with the Department for their release. Surely we cannot afford to pay our soldiers and sailors less than an adequate wage, and an adequate wage should be paid to all government employees, whether they be privates in the army or admirals of a fleet. For the Government to save money by oppressing its employees is a crime not only against the employees, but against all decent American citizens.

Of the sickly sentimentalists who support every cause where they are free to shed tears I have little to say. They remind me of the strange crowd that gathers at funerals. They do not know the deceased nor the family, but they derive a kind of salty delight in crowding into the church and weeping. They go home and report they had a perfectly delightful time, and "didn't the corpse look lovely!" I know of no cure for these people. Perhaps a brain specialist might be able to suggest one, provided he was able to find any brain to apply his remedy to.

The internationalist is also one who sympathizes with the bolshevistic tendencies of the times. He has a love affair with every country but his own. He loves all nations, but is loyal to no nation. He is the international *roué*. He certainly professed undying affection for the countries across the sea, but during the late war he went to the military prisons rather than fight to save them! *He obstructed in every manner possible every act of our Government. He refused to assist the boys across the sea.* He spread lying tales about all in positions of authority. He is absolutely, completely, and unequivocally *no good*.

Roosevelt covered his case very succinctly and properly when he said:

The professed internationalist usually sneers at nationalism, at patriotism, and at what we call Americanism. He bids us forswear our love of country in the name of love of the world at large. We nationalists answer that he has begun at the wrong end; we say that, as the world now is, it is only the man who ardently loves his country first who in actual practice can help any other country at all...

The best world-citizen is the man who first and foremost is a good citizen of his own country. Within our national limits I distrust any man who is as fond of a stranger as he is of his own family, and in international matters I even more keenly distrust the man who cares for other nations as much as for his own. I do not trust persons whose affections are so diffuse. There are men who look upon their wives or mothers or countries and upon other women and other countries with the same tepid equality of emotion. I do not regard these men as noble or broad-minded. I regard them as rotten.

An American who does not love his country more than any other country is not a good American. He is not a patriot. He is not an asset to our nation. He is a positive detriment. He is a great weeper, but a poor worker. He sympathizes, but never helps. Emerson said: "Love afar is spite at home." He is like unto the man who leaves an oasis in the desert to follow a mirage. His internationalism is polygamatic. The only citizen we can trust is the citizen who trusts his country. For one, I am not willing to allow the water in our national pool to be lowered to the level of the pool of other nations. We must not lower our national standard by chasing the will o' the wisp of internationalism. Our country should be run primarily for the benefit of the people of our country. We will in the future, as we have in the past, stand ready to relieve those in distress, but only by building up a strong nationalism will we ever be able to help any one. The good farmer does not benefit his poor neighbour farmer by allowing his fields also to grow up with weeds. I do not believe in watering our national stock and increasing the figures on the faces of the stock certificates, and pretending to ourselves that we have gained thereby. As a nation, we can and will enter into certain definite agreements and treaties with other governments, but we *must preserve our nationalism inviolate*.

Another cause of unrest and bolshevism is the presence here and there of discontented failures and delinquents. Many men become angry and resentful if the world does not take them at their own valuation. They then try to spread their discontent. Constitutionally and temperamentally unfit for success, they try to capitalize their failure. Until the formula is discovered that will make men and women uniform in ability they will have to go on their discontented way to the end. The doctrines of syndicalism have apparently a peculiar attraction for delinquents. The moron and the mattoid nearly always support such doctrines. Whenever any large number of I.W.W.'s were arrested for disturbing the peace, it was but necessary to look at them to realize that many of them were not only delinquents, but were physically and mentally unfit to battle with life. What to do with these mental and physical weaklings is one of the quandaries that confront all governments. They are, of course, easy prey for the mouthy talkers who, unable even to produce enough to buy a suit of clothes, talk learnedly of conducting the affairs of great nations.

Chapter Fourteen - Bolshevism Contrasted with Americanism

ALL history points to the fact that our country came into being, destined to be the place where the problems of working out a perfect freedom and liberty for all mankind should be solved through orderly evolution. I cannot believe that our country, with a past so full of splendid achievement; with its soil drenched with the blood of its heroic dead; with its ideals living, breathing, and pulsing in the hearts of millions, has at last reached the point on its short but momentous journey where its ideals and institutions, which have been created through travail, suffering, and sacrifice, shall cease to exist and be supplanted by an autocratic dictatorship of any class whatsoever. And yet, the events of the past few years must cause the student of life and history to consider well the real conditions of the United States of America and the effect of the propaganda of discontent and lawlessness.

When the thirteen little colonies declared their independence and defied Great Britain, we were in danger; again in 1812, when war came once more to curse the land, we faced disaster; in the 60's, when our nation divided and fought itself nigh unto death, we were sorely stricken, and when we embarked upon the great adventure and declared war against the foes of civilization, liberty, and freedom, we cast our birthright into the balance, unafraid. To-day, all that we strove for in the past — all the privileges — all the freedom — all the liberty and all the self-government which our heroes won by their sacrifice, stands in manifest and almost immediate jeopardy.

Every good man must abhor, every wise man condemn, any government which does not grant *equal justice* to *all its citizens.* A government founded on injustice may well be likened to a sea without water — a world without light — a home without love. Justice, freedom, and liberty are liv*ing things and not resounding words.* Justice cannot exist where there is class government; justice cannot exist where all men are not equal before the law; justice cannot exist under minority rule; justice cannot exist where people are not self-governed. The attacks made by syndicalism, etc., are simply mass attacks against the very fabric of our civilization.

Let us pause for a moment and consider our Government, our ideals, and our institutions, and contrast them with the doctrines and practices which the befooled and the knave would substitute.

The real American believes in putting more into the Government than he takes out of it;

The bolshevist wants to take more out than he puts in.

Americanism stands for liberty;

Bolshevism is premeditated slavery.

Americanism is a synonym of self-government;

Bolshevism believes in a dictatorship of tyrants.

Americanism means equality;

Bolshevism stands for class division and class rule.

Americanism is democracy;

Bolshevism is autocracy.

Americanism stands for orderly, continuous, never-ending progress;

Bolshevism stands for retrograding to barbaric government.

Americanism stands for law;

Bolshevism disdains law.

Americanism means love of your fellow man;

151

Bolshevism teaches and practises hatred and envy.

Americanism stands for hope;

Bolshevism stands for despair.

One is the philosophy of optimism;

The other, the practice and belief of pessimism.

Americanism is founded on family love and family life;

Bolshevism is against family life.

Americanism stands for one wife and one country;

Bolshevism stands for free love and no country.

Americanism means increased production and increased prosperity for all;

Bolshevism stands for destruction, restriction of output, and compulsory poverty.

An American believes in a strong national government; he is patriotic and loyal;

Bolshevists believe in destruction of nationalism, loyalty, and patriotism and the adoption of a sentimental, sickly, unworkable, skim-milk internationalism. Loving no country, they excuse themselves by saying they love all countries alike. Polygamous men have ever used the same excuse.

Americanism stands for the protection of private rights and property;

Bolshevism stands for the destruction of all private rights and the confiscation of all property.

Americanism believes in strength;

Bolshevism teaches premeditated weakness and inefficiency.

Americanism stands for preparedness and universal training;

Bolshevism would disarm and Chinafy our great people.

Americanism has taught and Americans have practised morality;

Bolshevism teaches and its votaries practise immorality, indecency, cruelty, rape, murder, theft, arson.

Americanism stands for God and good;

Bolshevism is against both God and good.

Americanism thrives on truth;

Truth destroys bolshevism.

Americanism conquers by reason;

Bolshevism cannot stand the light of reason.

Americanism has proven true by experience;

All experience has proven bolshevism false.

Americanism is success;

Bolshevism is failure.

Under our Government we have prospered, grown, become and remained free;

Under bolshevism, wherever tried, people have starved, suffered, become and remained slaves.

Every man and most women can vote in our country and every individual has one vote and one only;

Under bolshevism, many people cannot vote at all while others have but one vote to another man's 800.

Americanism rewards individual effort and toil;

Bolshevism rewards the loafer and robs the producer.

Americanism is great enough to be just and just enough to be great;

Bolshevism is always unjust and in its injustice only is great.

Americanism grants full and equal justice to all;

Bolshevism gives special privileges to some but justice to none.

Our countryside rings with happy song and laughter;

Russia, the bolshevists' paradise, knows neither happiness nor song.

Americanism means education, universal and free;

Bolshevism tends to static and degrading ignorance.

American institutions are founded on the solid rock of human rights;

Bolshevism softens its people into a pulp — a pulp without wrinkles, but also without a backbone.

The men who created and led America were believers in liberty and freedom and were willing to die for America.

The men who lead the bolsheviki are trying to revitalize the shifting shadows of an outgrown past and by coating the disastrous record with an enamel of lies, are trying to befool the people of the world.

Americanism is a substantial, living, breathing, functioning, successful ideal;

Bolshevism is as full of holes as a sponge, and has no ideals.

In spite of the failure of its practices wherever tried, the teachings and practices of Bolshevism have permeated the very fibre of great numbers of people. I cannot too often emphasize that bolshevism has always failed completely and overwhelmingly whenever tried. We have seen how it failed in France, and after a careful study of conditions in Russia we find that Russia is not free, is not prosperous, but is oppressed and poverty-stricken, and suffering from autocratic tyranny.

If bolshevism could succeed anywhere, it would have succeeded in Russia where industry and life are primitive; where the complex problems that confront a developed and civilized people are absent. Nearly every community in Russia was self-sustaining; 85 per cent, of the people where land tillers; there was but little industrial enterprise or commerce, and yet, even under these primitive conditions, *it has failed*. How much greater, more complete and disastrous the failure would be in this country can well be imagined. In the United States our development and interdependence is so complex that the stoppage of the railroads for a few days would bring untold suffering to our people. All the cogs of our enterprise must be in place or the machine will *stop*. We have ceased to be primitive. Our civilization may be compared to a fine chronometer — Russia's to a lumber wagon. If bolshevism cannot successfully run a lumber wagon, what likelihood that it could run a chronometer?

Bolshevism in Russia has survived after a fashion for some time. Bolshevism in America could not in the nature of things function with any degree of success for thirty days. And yet, bolshevism, I.W.W.'ism, One Big Unionism, etc., have had a marked detrimental effect on our people.

Bolshevism has made revolutionists of loyal men and women;

It has destroyed love of country in the hearts and minds of thousands;

It has made many efficient, contented, and well-paid workers inefficient, complaining fault finders;

It has gained converts and supporters in every state of the Union;

It has caused industrious men to become loafers on the job; it has fanned the flames of hatred and envy;

It has *invaded the loyal organizations and assemblages of labour and is fast destroying the morale of many of our workers.*

It is destroying the old progressive labour organizations. The American Federation of Labour and I, W. W.'ism are fighting to the death, while unrest, strikes, and sabotage exist as never before.

Following is the number of strikes that occurred in this country during each month of 1919 up to September: January, 105; February, no; March, 102; April, 134; May, 219; June, 245; July, 364; August, 308.

The strikes in July and August were twice as many as in July and August, 1918. Officials of the American Federation of Labour estimate that there are at this writing 2,000 strike situations, meaning strikes going on or imminent.

The above figures were taken from Stanley Frost's article in the New York *Tribune* of September 15, 1919. He agrees with my statement that there has been a "progressive and pronounced decline in the actual quantity of goods produced."

One of the causes of these strikes is the spread of the Bolshevist beliefs, and the consequent practices thereof.

These teachings have destroyed in the minds of thousands the desire to work and produce. They have made infidels of the God-fearing; they have made criminals of the law-abiding. Bolshevik leaders have planned the destruction not only of government, law and order, but also the destruction of the lives and reputations of all who oppose them. Bolshevism preaches violence, hatred, and revolution instead of peace, progress, and evolution. Lies, crimes, and force are the tools used.

Under one name or another it has impregnated the minds of a great number of the workers of our country with its doctrines of sabotage;

It has taught the false doctrine that *the less you do the more you should have;*

It has restricted production in many instances 50 per cent.;

It has taught men to loaf on the job and defraud not only their employer, but civilization and themselves, and it is my belief that it will put to the test our present form of government.

All this, and much more, has taken place in a few years in a country where the people themselves govern, and where the majority are able, by the exercise of their political rights, to do as they wish.

Perhaps the greatest crime of all that it has committed is the teaching of the false doctrine that restricted production means more wealth, whereas the most elementary student must realize that restricted production is premeditated poverty for all.

Our country has the greatest natural resources of any country on the globe, and yet *we are growing poorer daily.* Let us forget the dollar and instead of saying that so many dollars' worth of this and that has been produced, let us measure our wealth in tons, in yards, and with such real measures.

With practically our entire population at work, we are producing less per capita than at any time since modern machinery came to aid the toiler. In the shipyards of the Northwest, and in the factories, stickers are posted everywhere telling the men to do but six hours' work in an eight-hour day. As a matter of fact, thousands are doing but four hours' work in an eight-hour day, and could practically double their production in many instances if they desired. I have no doubt that this slowing up of production, to a greater or less degree, is true all over the United States. The employer of labour simply adds to the selling price of his product the extra cost of production, and it is passed on to the ultimate consumer, and finally reaches the worker who slacked on the job.

In our lumber camps barely 60 per cent, as much lumber is produced by a given crew as was produced several years ago, under very much poorer working conditions, and all the time the syndicalist fatuously and ignorantly believes that by this slacking and loafing he is accomplishing good for himself. Of course, as a matter of fact, if a workman cuts his production in half, either the price of his half must be doubled or his wages must be cut in two. If it requires two men to do the work that one man previously performed, in the final analysis the two men will only receive the sum previously received by the one who did the same work.

If I cultivate 160 acres of land and reap 20 bushels of wheat to the acre, 3,200 bushels of wheat are produced. If I cultivate but 80 acres of land, which produces 20 bushels of wheat to the acre, only 1,600 bushels of wheat have been produced, and the world is 1,600 bushels of wheat poorer regardless of the price I receive for the wheat. Nobody can subsist on the dollar mark, but the extra 1,600 bushels of wheat would feed a number of people for a long time.

There never was a time in the history of the world when production was more greatly needed than at present. The boxes and barrels and bins of the warehouses are practically empty. The amount of deposits in the banks does not measure prosperity. The amount of food, clothing, homes, etc., is the true measure. Sluggards, drones, shirks, and slackers become really criminals in the face of the needs of humanity. The only things that will bring prosperity, peace, and general well-being, are work and thrift. Without work, without production, chaos and anarchy must result. All the resolutions adopted, and all the laws passed, will not raise one bushel of grain. Idleness, at the present time, is a national crime. Semi-idleness is almost as bad. The world must either *go to work, or starve and freeze* — mere words will not feed or clothe the children. Dreams are sometimes pleasant, but no one could ever dream strong enough or long enough to produce a bushel of potatoes. He who makes two blades of grass grow where but one grew before is a benefactor to humanity. He who makes one blade of grass grow where two grew before is society's enemy.

Steeped in sophistry, men are striving to find some way of having and enjoying without working and producing. Time, the great logician, goes relentlessly on its way and proves over and over again that there is only one way. History, the great expounder, proves that there has never been but one way. Common sense tells us all, rich and poor, employer and employee, that there is but one way. *We must produce more — not less — in order to have more.* The division of the product may be a just subject for dispute, but the necessity for more production cannot be disputed. Every nation, every man, must realize this fundamental. Wealth is not a static thing. Food, clothing, and all wealth are produced by work applied to natural resources. It never has been and never can be produced otherwise. The more work that is applied to natural resources, the more wealth — the less work, the less wealth. I care not what the dollar value of production shows. It means nothing. I do care, however, what the bushel measure demonstrates. When we work 50 per cent, we become a 50-per-cent people. Let all production stop and in just a short time the saved-up wealth of the centuries fades away and disappears.

Wealth is an ever and constantly changing entity. It grows larger or smaller according to production. In all ism philosophy, work is looked upon as an evil while it is in fact the greatest blessing ever conferred on man. A people impregnated by the habit of work is irresistible. The greatest joy in life is creative work. Loafers are neither healthy, useful, nor happy. All cessation of work, whether by lockout or strike, is premeditated poverty.

How have the bolsheviki accomplished this destructive effect?

By the constant, everlasting advertisement of their false ideas through agitation.

By the spoken and written word.

By fanatical willingness to spend time and money promulgating their doctrines.

What have we done? What are we doing? What shall we do?

Shall we sit idly by and see things get worse?

Shall we "pass the buck"?

Shall we loll and dream and then have a terrific awakening? — or shall we play the man's part and adopt measures of cure?

I must again speak of the value of advertising truth.

I must again call your attention to the fact that a propaganda of lies will stand *unless it is answered by truths plainly and bluntly told.*

They have their propaganda and are using it; it is everywhere, in the farmhouse and in the mill; in the forest and in the factory; in the mouths of their voluble leaders, on the front pages of their papers and pamphlets.

156

Our propaganda, our truths, are hidden away in our hearts and minds. *We must tell the truth to remain free.* We must issue pamphlets. We must use the city press, country press, and the magazines. We must send speakers over the land. We must make the fight, and despite your complacent belief, dear reader, it is a real and not a sham fight. It is a fight for freedom an! peace and home and law and order and all that we hola dear.

Will you help? Will you do your share? Will you assist in every way possible." Will you forget *the "profits"* for a while and *help save your country?* If so, all will be well and we will win. If we shirk, if we slack, if we trim, if we compromise, we will lose, every last mother's son and daughter of us in this great land of ours, and the greatest losers will be *the very men who are being misled by the Red liars.*

Again I say, deport the anarchist, the bolshevist, the alien agitator. Americanize the alien; spend time and money and effort. We can do it — let's "go to it!" Deflate the currency, gradually and carefully. It will decrease the cost of living. Red employers must be disciplined. They must be made to do right. Red employees also must be punished. Both kinds of Reds *must do right or starve.* Pay all governmental and semi-governmental employees a living wage. If present officials won't do it, change them. It's our money, not theirs. *Advertise the truth about government everywhere and all the time.* Let us educate ourselves as well as everybody in this land. Refuse to admit any more immigrants except as *we select them and need them, and admit no man for a permanent stay who is not able, or does not wish, to become a citizen.*

Let us run the United States for the people of the United States!

It were well, at this time, to consider our assets and liabilities. At the year's close a wise business man takes an inventory. Let us do so.

We are all shareholders in that great enterprise, the United States of America. Let us hold a shareholders' meeting wherein we will discuss freely and frankly our balance sheet.

What are the assets of our country?

We have nearly two billion acres of land, of which only one acre in seven is under cultivation, and of which there are still two hundred and twenty-five million acres in the hands of the Government, as well as many more fertile millions undeveloped and non-producing in the hands of private individuals.

We have 265,000 miles of railroads, of which 260,000 miles are reasonably good roads. In other words, private capital has built, for profit, this vast extent of public highways. The railroads of the United States would go around the world ten times, and then there would be enough remaining to more than traverse our entire boundary line.

We have four thousand two hundred and thirty-one billions of tons of unmined coal in the United States and Alaska. Canada comes second with one thousand three hundred and sixty-one billion tons, and China third, but the unmined coal in all the countries of the world outside our own amounts to but three thousand six hundred and fifty-two billion tons. We have over five hundred billion more tons of unmined coal than all the rest of the world.

157

In 1810, we produced fifty thousand tons of pig iron; in 1850, half a million tons; in 1900, twenty-four million tons, and in 1915, thirty million tons. The total production of pig iron for the world in 1910 was sixty-five and a half million tons, while in 1915, the total production was three million tons less, or sixty-two million. Under normal conditions, we produce more than 45 per cent, of this great basic mineral.

In 1810, we had one hundred and twenty-three thousand manufacturing establishments; in 1850, two hundred and fifty thousand; in 1900, the progress of consolidation had reduced this number to two hundred and seven thousand, and to-day, we have but two hundred and seventy-five thousand such establishments, or about the same number that we had forty years ago.

I speak of the land, as in the final analysis, food is our prime necessity and properly developed our lands can and will support many times our present population. Our farming has, to a large extent, been simply soil-mining, until the impoverished soil has resulted in a small crop, or no crop; nothing having been put back onto the land to feed it, despite all that was taken from it.

I speak of our railroads, because the distribution of commodities becomes more and more complex, necessary, and important. I speak of our unmined coal as a great resource, because this stored-up sunshine of the ages means that we should take the lead in all manufacturing industries in time to come. Coal means heat, life, action.

Our undeveloped waterpower cannot be too highly appreciated. The time will surely come when the water that runs from the mountains to the seas will, in constantly increasing ratio, turn the busy wheels of industry and give out light, heat, and warmth to our people.

Our pools of petroleum hidden away through all the centuries, hundreds of feet below the surface of the earth, become more and more needed as the development of the gas engine takes the place of older methods of producing power.

And our iron. Think of the vast stores of iron still concealed amidst the rocks and clay of our sub-soils! We have reached the age of iron and without it no nation can become either very prosperous or powerful.

But we have one huge asset not heretofore mentioned, and that is, one hundred and ten millions of free, progressive, productive people — people who have in the past, and will I trust continue in the future, to produce more per capita than any other people on the face of the earth.

We suffered much during the late war, and yet but little in comparison with the warring countries of Europe. An Italian statistician has carefully compiled the losses resulting from the great conflict and he states that it will take, under normal conditions, ten years for England to regain her lost man power; fifteen years for Germany; thirty-three years for Italy, and sixty-six years for beautiful France.

We have the most efficient and best labour power on earth. The leaders of thought, of industry, of action and progress of every kind in Europe, the graduates of the great universities, lie dead on Flanders fields — but the loss of our thinkers, our planners, and our captains, while they did their share, and their full share, during our part in the war, was very small in comparison with that of the other countries. Our workers are alive. Millions of the workers of the other countries, whether allies or enemies, are dead. Our leaders, too, are alive, while their leaders are dead. We have the men and the brains, as well as the largest aggregation of capital of any country in the world to-day. The future belongs to us.

We have but one possible liability confronting us, and that is industrial and civil strife. We need fear no foreign competition. Not only were millions of the men of Europe wiped out by war or disease, but millions more have adopted and put into practice syndicalism and sabotage, with consequent restriction of production, making it impossible for these great nations to compete on equal terms with us with all our natural resources and, I trust, the incentive to produce.

The coal miners of Great Britain refuse to mine coal and we ship millions of tons to Italy, Switzerland, and other countries. The peasants of Russia are not raising sufficient food for themselves; hence our markets for food products are world-wide. We can sell bicycles in London across the street from the factory located there, and undersell the local factory. We can, if we will, control the foreign trade of the world.

At the commencement of the war we had few or no ships of our own to carry our produce. To-day we have many ships, and are building more and more.

We have a government truly representative of the people themselves — a government under which all have an equal opportunity. If we, the people of this great country, founded on the principles of freedom and liberty, will unite, will go to work, will cooperate, will preach and practise the doctrine of thrift and work, we may embark upon the greatest era of prosperity any country has ever known in all history.

If we will but cooperate and settle our disputes by agreement, instead of by force and violence, all may receive the greatest blessings. This is my country, it is your country. Its government is our Government, and we must fight to the last against the domination of our Government and our country by any one class.

Whenever the majority of our people desire to change or amend any part of our structure, they can do it. Our Government is a government by majorities. No minority must ever be allowed to control its affairs. No class, whether bankers or plumbers, must have a greater voice in its affairs than the Constitution and laws grant them. We must cooperate and conquer ignorance, poverty, and injustice. We must build on the foundations laid down by our ancestral fathers. Our great experiment in government must not be allowed to fail. Our flag must not be stained red. Our children must be taught the truth, at home and in the schools. Our grown men and women must be made to reahze the beauty, the utility, the superiority of our Government. In the near future — perhaps sooner than many of us believe — our solidarity, our loyalty, and our unity will be tested. When that time comes, God grant that you and I, and all of us, may have fulfilled our duty to our country and to one another.

We must know the truth — and carry it to every man, woman, and child in our land. With the truth in the hearts and souls of all of us we need have no fear, for truth is mighty and will prevail. The man of truth will dissipate the mists of falsehood and the right, the fair, the square, and the loyal will be successful. To believe otherwise would be to doubt God and good and to question the ultimate happiness and peace of humanity.

Again I say: This is our country and our Government. Let us cherish its institutions and ideals — let us stand by its laws; let us work for it, live for it, and — if necessary — *die for it*.

> Sail on, O Ship of State!
> Sail on, O Union, strong and great!
>   Humanity with all its fears,
>   With all the hopes of future years,
> Is hanging breathless on thy fate!

THE END

www.ingramcontent.com/pod-product-compliance
Lightning Source LLC
Chambersburg PA
CBHW051829040426
42447CB00006B/434